Recovery Revolution:

A Social Recovery Blueprint for Optimal Mental Health

Recovery Revolution:

A Social Recovery Blueprint for Optimal Mental Health

Paul F. Rashid MD

P2 Productions

ⓊP2 Productions

Published by P2 Productions LLC
Charleston WV, USA

PaulRashidMD.com

Cover design by Paul Rashid MD and Nicholas Shaheen MD
Back Photo by Donald Fidler MD

ISBN 978-0-9988387-0-0 paperback
Library of Congress Control Number: 2017906495

First printing

Medical Disclaimer

The contents of this book are intended for informational purposes and education of the reader. It is not a substitute for medical, psychiatric or psychological evaluation, diagnosis, or treatment. Please, always discuss your medical conditions and treatments with your healthcare professionals. Please note, the stories in this book are true, but all names except for my own, have been changed to protect each individual's identity.

Dedication

This book is dedicated to those who have suffered from mental illnesses, the brave persons who have pioneered the recovery movement, and for those courageous individuals who are setting off on their journey of recovery.

Contents

Forward

By Donald Fidler MD

A tenet of medical education is for practitioners to become life-long learners. Dr. Paul Rashid is a physician, who boldly embraces life-long learning as he embarks on delightful journeys off traditional paths, and returns to combine new visions with traditional ideas. Dr. Rashid peers beyond the labeling of psychiatric diagnoses, and avalanche of psychiatric medications of traditional practice, and he asks the essential questions, "What would true recovery from mental disorders and/or stress look like, and how would people arrive there?" He searches for answers for himself, bravely sharing in his book about his own recovery from panic, and he searches for answers for his patients.

Dr. Paul Rashid combined knowledge and experience from numerous spheres: his medical and psychiatric education, his practicing in the Veterans Hospital mental health system, his working as a psychiatrist in numerous communities, his interest in medical history, cultures, his joy of international travel, and his inquisitive pursuit for studying how people can live healthy lives. The result is a splendid self-help book entitled, *Recovery Revolution*. His transcending work clarifies complex, cutting-edge medical and psychiatric research and holistic medical ideas as digestible treats for easy public reading.

Research literature reveals significant deficits in medical education. Medical students are not taught to educate patients about the critical importance of personal-social-spiritual growth, healthy nutrition, and about the powers of mind-over-body interventions. Dr. Rashid brilliantly weaves these themes throughout his masterful book, presenting story-fashioned examples.

I have been one of Dr. Paul Rashid's psychiatry teachers, a professor who practiced and taught psychiatry for thirty-three years, when he asked me to read his rough draft. Before I completed reading his book, I already found myself applying his ideas for my own health. I wasted no time in sharing his ideas with my friends and family members, who continue to thank me for sharing Dr. Rashid's life changing advice.

Thank you for your enthusiasm, your compassion, and your willingness to share your found ideas with all of us on this planet. We are better. We are grateful.

Author Biography

Hello, my name is Paul Rashid. I am a board-certified and recovery-oriented psychiatrist who is fiercely committed to guiding people with mental stress to achieve mental health recovery so they can reclaim their lives, stop being ruled by mental illness, and live to their highest functional ability.

With over 10 years of clinical experience working with amazing clients who share similar worries and concerns, I have guided many people to achieve remarkable success.

My path to becoming a psychiatrist started at an early age with my interest in the human story. I have always been fascinated by psychology, human behavior, and the human mind; I believe the human mind is mankind's final frontier. I was a kid who loved comic books, movies, and books—fiction and nonfiction alike—these works share the common theme of the human story. Psychiatry is my true calling and a very fulfilling career. It blends my passion for science and the human condition. What excites me about recovery work is knowing that you don't have to continue to be a prisoner to mental illness. Recovery is possible!

Most people receiving traditional psychiatric treatment receive only medication. Some are lucky enough to also benefit from talk therapy. I am introducing an additional, third level to mental health treatment by adding social recovery, which gives you the most powerful advantage and empowers you in your treatment of mental illness.

Social recovery is an effective treatment, but because it was born out of the civil rights and social movement, it is not emphasized in the classic medical psychiatric model. My goal is to give you the tools you will need for recovery. You can feel confident allowing me to act as a guide for you and your loved ones to overcome these problems.

I was born and raised in West Virginia. I have a Lebanese heritage and was raised with strong family values, middle eastern culture and, of course, the amazing Mediterranean cuisine!

My medical education began at the Joan C. Edwards School of Medicine at Marshall University. My psychiatry specialization was completed through West Virginia University, and I had the honor of serving as Chief Resident during my senior year of residency in psychiatry.

After about a year of practicing psychiatry at a state hospital, I decided to pursue an additional year of training, this time in a fellowship focusing exclusively on psychosocial rehabilitation and recovery for severe mental illness through the La Jolla San Diego, California, VA healthcare system.

This is where my interest in recovery began and continues to this day. Since then, I have been helping people struggling with every form of mental illness. I am American Board Certified in Psychiatry and I have clinical work experience in both outpatient clinics and in VA medical centers and community hospitals.

One thing that might surprise you to know is that I am in recovery from panic and anxiety. My journey through medical school, residency, and clinical work as a psychiatrist has been filled with continuous challenges, and I use daily psychological practices to manage my stress level.

In a world of ever increasing complexity and uncertainty, I am proud of you for taking the first step towards your recovery! It would be my pleasure to help guide you to achieve the life you imagine in our recovery work together.

Acknowledgments

I would like to thank my family, friends, colleagues, and mentors:

- First and foremost, the psychologists and psychiatrists from the San Diego, California, VA Psychosocial Rehabilitation for Severe Mental Illness Fellowship:
  - Eric Granholm PhD, David Lehman MD, Christine Rufener PhD, Colin Depp PhD, Demtri Perivolitis PhD, Sidney Zisook MD, David Printz MD, Daniel Brockett MD, and Robert Gorney MD.
  - My three colleagues who completed the fellowship program with me and aided in my understanding of psychology, vocational rehabilitation, and recovery: Ashley Wynne Pape PhD, Laura Carpenter Stull PhD, and Nicholas Coniaris.
- I am indebted to my family:
  - My father, Richard C. Rashid MD, who has been an amazing role model for me, not only in medicine, but with his incredible work ethic, accomplishments, and being the embodiment of a true gentleman.
  - My mother, Eleanor, a superwoman who shows her love through acts of selfless giving every single day.
  - My oldest brother, Charles, who always looked out for me when I was growing up, and continues to this day. My brother, Mitchell Rashid MD, and sister, Nicole Rashid Bown MD, who both led the way for my medical education. My Brother-in-law, Paul Bown MD, whose background in both literature and medicine offered a well-rounded final review.
- My friends who have supported me during my medical training, early career, and personal growth, and who also encouraged my writing:
  - Vincent Burskey JD, Jimmy Mali MD, and Stephanie Hilton.
  - More recently: Anil Bajnath MD, Kathy Louvaris ARNP, Kelly Sunshine ARNP, and Linda Chambers RN-BC.
  - Andrea Arco and Arco + Associates. Andrea and I have been friends since junior high school. She was my honorary English mentor then, and I still rely on her literary guidance over twenty years later.

- My psychiatry and psychology mentors:
  - Including, but not limited to: James Stevenson MD, Martin Kommor MD, Ryan Finkenbine MD, T.O. Dickey MD, Carl R Sullivan MD, Dianne Trumbull MD, Toni Goodykoontz MD, Daniel Elswick MD, James Peykanu MD, Justin Petri MD, Wanhong Zheng MD, Eric Rankin PhD, Scott Pollard MD, and Marc Haut PhD.
  - All the psychiatrists and residents with whom I have had the great privilege to work, interact, and learn from throughout the years.
  - John Linton PhD and Barry Fisher MD who provided generous suggestions and guidance for *Recovery Revolution*.
  - Don Fidler MD who has fostered my creative endeavors since residency and was an exceptional support during the writing and publishing of *Recovery Revolution*.
- I am grateful for the countless friends, family and co-workers, who provided invaluable feedback and unconditional support for *Recovery Revolution*.

Lastly, I would like to thank my virtual mentors that have educated me from afar via books, documentaries, podcasts, webinars, and online resources. I have listed in alphabetical order according to their "middle name":

David "Avacado" Wolfe, Tony "Awaken the Giant Within" Robbins, Lisa "Aware Show" Garr, Bruce "Biologist" Lipton, Donna "Body Ecology" Gates, Dave "Bulletproof" Asprey, Elyn "Center Cannot Hold" Saks, my fellow West Virginian Jack "Chicken Soup for the Soul" Canfield, James "Choose Yourself" Altucher, Joseph "Control Your Health" Mercola, Dr. Mark "Eat Fat Get Thin" Hyman, Joe "Fat, Sick and Nearly Dead" Cross, Joe "Fear Factor" Rogan, John "Food Revolution" Robbins, Rhonda "FoundMyFitness" Patrick, Tim "Four Hour Workweek" Ferriss, Dr. Joel "GBOMBS" Fuhrman, Dr. David "Grain Brain" Permutter, Brian "It's Your Hour" Rashid, Dr. Drew "Loveline" Pinsky, Marc "Psychology of Eating" David, Patricia "Recovery" Deegan PhD, Dr. Wayne "Self-Help" Dyer, Mike "Self-Made Man" Dillard, Hans "Spiritual Teacher" King, another fellow West Virginian Morgan "Super Size Me" Spurlock, Christine "Transformational Author" Kloser, Kay "Unquiet Mind" Jamison, Dr. Pedram "Urban Monk" Shojai, JJ "Virgin Diet" Virgin, Dr. Daniel "Warrior's Way" Amen, and Dr. Josh "Wellness" Axe.

PART I

Introduction to Recovery Concepts

Who is This Book For?

Anyone, and everyone, especially those struggling with psychological distress and have a desire to improve how they feel and function. As you will understand by the conclusion of this book, if you are breathing you are in recovery. Readers will learn how to evaluate and improve their social abilities while ensuring maximum functioning, in spite of any stressor. Think of recovery as an individualized approach that you initiate for your mental and physical health. Get ready to discover your road to recovery.

How to Use This Book

In the first part of this book, I will introduce myself and share my personal experience with mental illness. We'll rediscover our body's inherit ability to heal. Then briefly review humankind's past struggle with mental health issues and why we are living in the best time in history to be addressing problems with depression, fluctuating moods, mania, anxiety, problematic behaviors, and mental stressors. We will define social recovery and explore the bio-psycho-social formulation. Then, I will offer several important foundations of recovery.

In Part II, I present my Wheel of Recovery. Visual representations help increase the rate of learning new ideas. I believe this visual representation will help you more deeply understand recovery.

In the third, and final part, I will introduce the blueprint of social recovery, which I have divided into 10 elements. Here, we will delve into each component of recovery. These chapters may be read in any order, but I have organized them into the most basic needs, progressing to physical health, and then finishing with more complex elements. You may read them in chronological order or start with a section that you have been struggling with or want to tackle first. You can then refer back to any chapter for future review. Social interventions work on a number of levels, but a streamlined explanation is that socialization decreases stress through a variety of emotional, mental, and physical mechanisms. As you build your mental health recovery, you will be adding social activities to your life. Each undertaking will be selected by you. There is no right or wrong pursuit, as long as it benefits you and causes no harm to others. You may find repeated readings of this book helpful as your comprehension of recovery improves.

Some chapter end with questions or comments that are meant to jumpstart implementing recovery elements into your life. I have created a Recovery Revolution Worksheet, which collects all the questions from each chapter listed in a word document. I have made it accessible for free to anyone on my website. Simply go to the "Resources" tab PaulRashidMD.com or scan the QR Code to download and print.

Although most self-development books do not include bibliographies, I have chosen to do so. I want to ensure that everyone is aware of the scientific nature of my discussion, as well as allowing anyone the ability to reference the source materials.

This is only a guide, there is no one way to recover. There is no perfect person or perfect recovery. Life is a journey; I invite you to live your life to the fullest.

Chapter 1:

My Journey through Mental Illness

My first dealings with mental illness were personal and preceded my psychiatric training. While I was a second-year medical student, I was met with a very powerful and overwhelming force, panic.

I had planned a fun weekend for myself in the midst of a busy medical school semester. I was preparing for an upcoming medical board exam and needed a break. The board exam is one of the most challenging exams in medical school. Preparing for it is no small feat as it tests all information learned in the preceding two years. As a reward for my hard work, and a little vacation from the high level of stress, I planned on spending a weekend at one of my favorite past times, Comic Con. So, I set out on the five-hour drive from Huntington, West Virginia to Charlotte, North Carolina.

There I was, surrounded by thousands of comic books and fellow fans, happily flipping through comic books, jumping from table to table, row after row. I had skipped lunch because time flies when you're having so much fun. Besides, I wanted to make it through as many booths as I could before the end of the day. Suddenly, I began to have an odd sensation.

I became light-headed and dizzy. I starting panting, my fingers were tingling, my heart was pounding out of my chest, my vision faded, and I feared that I might be having a heart attack. The intensity of these experiences was sharp and shot through my body. If you were to compare the sensation to the volume of a stereo, it was on full blast! My thoughts were spiraling out of control and I felt like I was going to die right there on the convention center floor.

I slumped to the ground, smack dab in the middle of the convention aisle. I was in survival mode, just trying to feel grounded while taking deep breaths. Someone helped me to the convention medical technician who checked my vital signs, including blood pressure, pulse, and blood sugar, all of which were normal. Although the medical technician told me I was medically "fine," I continued to feel this overwhelming tension. These thoughts continued to consume my mind and loomed like a cloud. I was trembling on the inside. This feeling followed me, even after leaving the convention center.

I did not feel safe driving the five-hour commute home, so I booked a hotel room. All night, I continued to have this extremely uneasy chest tightness and shaking all over. I feared another intense episode would recur. I couldn't shake the tormenting thought that I was experiencing some medical heart condition.

I wasn't sure what was happening, or what might happen next. I was so worried that I was only able to get two or three hours of restless sleep. The next day I was tired yet on edge. It was an awful feeling. I got home safely, but I was so tense my knuckles were white from squeezing the steering wheel the entire trip home.

First thing Monday morning, I scheduled an appointment with my primary care physician. All my routine blood tests, including blood count, electrolyte chemistries, and thyroid tests came back normal.

My doctor informed me of his diagnosis – a panic attack. He gave me brief counseling on anxiety, handed me two prescriptions to be taken as needed for panic, and referred me to a talk therapist. I followed up with him a few weeks later, having not gone to the talk therapist.

Looking back at his treatment, I believe he handled my case very well, and he was correct to refer me for a talk therapist appointment, yet I never made the appointment. Unfortunately, this is something I see all too often in the clinical setting; people often skip making that appointment out of fear of talking about and confronting their issues, fear of stigma and labeling, scheduling conflicts, or lack of insurance or funds to pay.

In spite of the added challenges anxiety has caused in my life, it might have made me a better person. I tend to be cautious before making important decisions and actions. It may even help me be a better physician, as I tend to make thorough evaluations and double check my work.

Ultimately I tackled my problem on my own, with a little help from my medical and psychiatric education, and a whole lot of trial and error. I continued to have panic attacks for years, but less frequently and never to the intensity of the first one.

Now in the rare event that I begin to feel panic I am able to take a mental step back, take several deep breaths, and stop the panic attack without anyone even noticing I'm in distress. Please note, this is after years of practicing and mastering deep breathing. I am proud to say that I am in recovery from my panic disorder. Just as I have found healing, so can you.

Unlike me, you don't have to figure out your recovery on your own. You hold the keys to your mental health recovery, but I hope to be a guiding light to help illuminate your individual recovery path.

Chapter 2:

Heal Thyself

"Health is a state of complete physical, mental, and social well-being and not merely the absence of disease or infirmity"

Health as defined by the World Health Organization

There is a modern belief in western society that pills cure people. I previously held this belief. I would frequently get sore throats when I was younger. My mother would take me to the throat specialist and I would be prescribed antibiotics. I still remember the pink, liquid bubble gum flavored elixir. As I got older and was able to swallow pills, I graduated to the three times a day, ten-day course of antibiotics. It wasn't until medical school that I learned some antibiotics don't kill bacteria, your body attacks and destroys bacteria and viruses. Your body's immune system is fully capable of combating illness. Antibiotics work a variety of ways. Some are "bactericidal" which results in killing the bacteria. Others are "bacteriostatic" which interferes with the bacteria's ability to replicate, in turn allowing your body to fight the remaining organisms more quickly. Medications are important and must be discussed with your doctor, but I just want to emphasize that your body has an innate ability to heal itself.

Psychiatrists and talk therapists provide powerful, sometimes lifesaving tools. These tools can give you the boost you need to cross the threshold towards mental well-being. But healing starts with you, you hold the keys to your recovery. You need to learn which keys open the locks, and only you can turn the key. The keys are located in the "toolbox" of social recovery. My 10 elements of recovery will guide your way and help you create and navigate your social recovery.

Chapter 3:

What is Mental Illness?

Diagnosis

What is mental illness? Many find this question difficult to answer, unclear, fearful, or just plain mysterious. Anyone who has taken an introduction to psychology course will have learned about "psychopathology." In medical school, physicians learn about disease states, or "pathology." Normally, we express ranges of emotional and physiologic states including joy, sadness, grief, and anxiety. Emotions, in and of themselves, are normal and part of the full human experience. It is when they last for extended periods of time that they can become hazardous. Emotional problems can affect an individual's social functioning, and can also have a direct negative impact on an individual's brain.

We have all experienced sadness, but when the sadness persists longer than hours or days it is classified as clinical depression. Joy is a blissful experience, but has the ability to destroy a person's life if it manifests as a manic episode. Anxiety and hypervigilance can ensure your safety in a life-threatening circumstance, but may evolve into panic disorder or post-traumatic stress disorder when our body experiences physiologic "fight or flight" symptoms in the absence of actual danger.

The classic psychiatric textbook called *The Diagnostic and Statistical Manual of Mental Disorders* (DSM) requires that "symptoms cause clinically significant distress or impairment in social, occupational, or other areas of functioning" for any psychiatric diagnosis. We will see dysfunction time and time again in this book related to impaired social functioning.

Rates of Mental Illness

No one is immune from mental illness; we are all potentially at risk. The National Institute of Mental Health reports that of American adults, 18% will experience anxiety each year, 28% will experience anxiety at some point in their lifetime, and 10% of American adults will experience a mood disorder each year, and 20% will experience a mood disorder in their lifetime. Of note women are 50-60% more likely than men to experience anxiety and mood disorders. Only 37% of people with anxiety disorders and 51% of the people experiencing mood disorders will receive treatment.[1,2] Additionally, the *World Health Organization lists depression as the leading cause of disability worldwide* as well as a major contributor to the global burden of disease.[3] The Greek philosopher, Aristotle, used a term "Eudemonia," which translates to mean happiness, well-being, or human flourishing. One study found that less than 20% of Americans are flourishing. That is less than 2 out of every 10 Americans.[4] The take-away from these numbers is that this is a huge problem and you are not the only person suffering!

Again, it is when the symptoms persist that dysfunction develops. Although some of the DSM time frames are arbitrary, they are indicators of persistent impairment. For example, depression is diagnosed after symptoms have endured a minimum of 2 weeks. Post-traumatic stress disorder requires ongoing symptoms for greater than a month. A diagnosis for schizophrenia requires significant impairment and symptoms for 6 months. I think it is noteworthy to mention that many times I have evaluated persons that have never been diagnosed or treated and the symptoms have been ongoing for months or even years before initiation of treatment. This is important because untreated illness has harmful effects on the brain itself.

Mental Illness and Brain Imaging

Numerous studies that measure areas of volume in the brain using magnetic resonance imaging (MRI) have repeatedly demonstrated that psychiatric disorders cause loss of brain tissue in specific anatomical regions.

Persons with untreated first episode major depressive disorder were found to have reduced volumes in anatomic areas in the brain when compared to a healthy control population.[5] Additional findings in those diagnosed with major depressive disorder have multiple areas of brain shrinkage or atrophy.[6] Interestingly, those depressed individuals treated with antidepressants had certain brain areas return to normal size as compared to those left untreated. This finding suggests that antidepressants help reverse the underlying anatomical brain deficits of depression.[7] Depressed persons with not previous antidepressant treatment also had decreased brain volume. Those individuals that were then treated with antidepressants had a subsequent improvement in these areas. This again shows the benefits of antidepressant treatment.[8]

Brain images in persons diagnosed with obsessive-compulsive disorder (OCD) were also found to have gray matter brain atrophy. Those treated with either Prozac or cognitive behavioral therapy demonstrated reversal of brain shrinkage in this same area. Said another way, regardless of treatment, whether it is talk therapy or selective serotonin reuptake inhibitor (SSRI) medication, both treatment modalities improved brain anatomy.[9]

It is important to note that these studies do not explain causation. That is to say we do not know if the psychiatric disorder causes brain atrophy or if this atrophy is a result of the underlying disorder. There continues to be a large amount of new brain research every year and scientists continue to research more advanced and precise treatments for mental disorders.

What does it all Mean?

These findings are important, because they help to clearly connect the severity of mental illness and brain pathology. *Mental disorders are brain disorders.* For example, depression is not something you can "talk yourself out of," just as one cannot talk themselves out of a measurable physical finding such as the low bone density found in osteoporosis.

The well-known Framingham Heart Study found that those with depression have a 50% increased risk of developing dementia, which is a serious and progressive brain degeneration with impaired memory.[10] Another study demonstrated repeated severe episodes of depression increase the individual's risk of developing dementia.[11]

These depression findings suggest important treatment considerations. Some would recommend aggressive antidepressant treatment to reverse the serious brain findings of depression and future risk of developing dementia.

However, a hopeful sign is that one of the root causes of depression is inflammation in the body. This is good news because you can make active changes in your lifestyle to reduce this inflammation, therefore reducing the risk and severity of depression. Lifestyle modifications include: eating a nutritionally dense diet, physical exercise, reducing weight, abstaining from smoking, correcting gut micro-flora with probiotics, improving sleep, and treating vitamin D deficiency.[12] We explore these topics and more in chapter 14 which covers physical health.

The bottom line is that one in five American adults will experience a mental health condition in their lifetime and over half will receive no treatment. Psychiatric disorders occur when the normal range of emotions persist longer than expected, with resulting impaired social functioning. Brain imaging using MRI technologies in various psychiatric diagnoses, including both depression and OCD, demonstrates brain volume reduction or shrinkage that is reversed by either talk therapy or antidepressant medication therapy. Mental illnesses are brain disorders. There is evidence to suggest aggressive treatment for depression not only reduces the symptoms of depression, but also treats the underlying cerebral abnormalities and decreases the risk of developing severe dementia. There continues to be research and hope for medical and technological advancements in mental health treatment in the future. You don't have to wait, because you have the power to take an active role with healthy lifestyle and social recovery interventions to reduce psychological distress.

Chapter 4:

A Brief History of Mental Illness

Earliest Documented Psychiatric Conditions

Mental illnesses have been described in some of the oldest written documents of mankind. Circa 1550 BC, the ancient Egyptian Ebers Papyrus papers describe depression and dementia. Ancient Indian Ayurveda Scriptures reference emotional states. These texts indicate that witchcraft or body fluid imbalances caused such states. Ayerveda suggests causes are due to poor diet, broken relationships between gods and other authoritative persons, and extreme fear or happiness. Ayerveda treatments included use of herbs, ointment, charms, prayer, emotional persuasion, and shocking the person. The Inner Canon of the Yellow Emperor is the fundamental Chinese medicine text and dates back to 475 BC. The Chinese text explains mechanisms of mental illness with an emphasis on the relationship between body organs and emotions. The symptoms were thought to originate from an imbalance between Yin and Yang energies and treated with herbs and acupuncture. Hippocrates, a Greek physician well-known as the "Father of Modern Medicine" lived from 460-370 BC. He classified many mental conditions including melancholia, mania, paranoia, and epilepsy. Celsus, a Roman physician, described diet, bloodletting, drugs, talk therapy, exorcism, incantations, restraints, starvation, stoning, and beating as treatments to restore sanity. Several Greek and Roman philosophers and physicians, including Celsus, believed that music treated emotional ills.

The Hebrew Bible, or Old Testament, contains passages describing mood disorders in both Job and King Saul in the Psalms of David. Here mental illnesses were caused by an impaired relationship between God and the individual. Arab texts discuss the connection between the brain and mind, as well as spiritual and mystic meaning of disorder. Some Arabian

17

and Islamic mythology blamed mental illness on possession by a Jinn or genie. Sometimes individuals were beaten to exorcise the genie. The first psychiatric hospitals and insane asylums were built in the Middle East in the 8th century. The European Middle Ages theorized imbalances in the four humors, with treatments that included purges, bloodletting, and whipping. If you were lucky to survive the witch-hunts of Colonial North America and Early Modern Europe, you may have only been subject to jail or the "madhouse." Those suffering from mental illness were thought of as wild animals. Harsh treatment, whippings, and chain restraints were viewed as therapeutic. Horrifying to fathom today, the London Bedlam asylum once charged bystanders to view inmates for entertainment!

History is filled with stories of those suffering from mental illness. Treatments were extremely limited which can be seen by the extremes to which people went to treat these conditions. The most common intervention was being confined to asylums. This would result in the individual being removed from society as well as having their basic human rights stripped away. These were the dark ages of mental illness treatment.[13]

Moral Treatment

Fortunately, the start of ethical treatment for those suffering mental illness began in France in the late 1700s. One of the first physicians to revolutionize mental illness treatment was Dr. Philippe Pinel, who was influenced by Jean-Baptiste Pussin, an "Ex-Patient." Together they created the humane treatment movement of those suffering in asylums, now called "Moral Treatment." An early American pioneer was Dorothea Dix, a mental health advocate in the late 1840s. She documented the poor condition of the mentally ill, where persons were caged, chained, naked, and beaten with rods. Ms. Dix actually lobbied state legislatures and the United States Congress to reform the mental treatment which resulted in building the early North American State Hospitals. Unfortunately, by the 20th century, asylums had become overpopulated, misused, and poorly maintained. The psychiatric asylum and "institutionalization" era ended starting in the 1950s with the advent of psychiatric medications. Today, psychiatric hospitalizations are short term. Average length of stay is around a week, sometimes a little longer, and intended for crisis stabilization. Extended length psychiatric hospitalization is uncommon and reserved for court ordered treatment or those suffering from the most severe and persistent symptoms.

The 1950s kicked off the Monoamine Theory of mental illness. This theory proposes that mental disorders are caused by variations in specific neurotransmitters such as serotonin, norepinephrine, and dopamine. Beginning with the antipsychotic medications in the 1950s and then subsequent medications for anxiety and depression, the most debilitating illnesses and burdens of disease around the globe had effective treatments. Consider this; anxiety affects one in four people and depression affects one in five people during their lifetime. Because of these medications, those suffering from severe symptoms are now treated. They regained their ability to live independently and left mental asylums, a process called deinstitutionalization.

Recovery and the Civil Rights Movement

During my psychiatric training, I had learned about the psychiatric deinstitutional shift that started in the 1960s using outpatient treatment and medication. This was made partially possible by the new revolution in psychiatric medications, specifically antipsychotic medication. This shift was to be financially supported by the federal government but this endeavor was never fully funded and local county mental health facilities continue to struggle with underfunding.

I was unaware of the civil rights movement impact on mental health until my psychosocial rehabilitation fellowship. A result of the civil rights movement included The Rehabilitation Act of 1973 Section 504, which created and extended civil rights to reasonable accommodations to children and adults with disabilities in education and work. In 1990 The Americans with Disabilities Act, which is commonly abbreviated as ADA, made the additional requirements for employers to provide reasonable accommodations to employees with disabilities and also imposed accessibility requirements to public facilities. These legislations are the reason why we have sidewalks with ramps for wheelchairs and why we have Braille signs for the visually impaired. Yet, ironically, almost five decades later we're still fighting for the recovery and rehabilitation of persons suffering from symptoms of mental illness.

The traditional psychiatric model is based on the medical model of mental illness. The "Social Recovery" model developed from the community and individual level as persons began writing narratives describing themselves as "recovered" or "in recovery." These two models were created separately; as a result they were never integrated. I hope to bridge the gap, so that both models will be prescribed and used together.

Mental Illness Stigma

The stigma of mental disorders has been demonstrated by ancient societies' attempts to treat, and at times discard, those afflicted. The "mental hygiene" movement originated in the U.S. in the 19th century. Its goal was to prevent insanity via public health and clinics.[2] The social stigma associated with mental health disorders continues to be a problem. Stigma of mental illness may have developed for biological and evolutionary reasons from the primal drive to persevere and protect the family unit. "Us versus them" is a mindset that tribes have utilized for millennia to survive. Today, it's a barrier that keeps some persons from seeking treatment. It can be rooted in anger and fear, causes harm, is discriminating and prevents healing. Although western civilization has shown the greatest reduction, this still persists.

In 1999, the U.S. Surgeon General said, "Powerful and pervasive, stigma prevents people from acknowledging their own mental health problems, much less disclosing them to others." One study found that mental illness was a bigger barrier to employment than having a physical disability.[14]

Reducing Stigma

What perpetuates stigma? Fear and lack of education. What is the solution to overcome stigma? Open communication and education.

People such as John F. Kennedy, the British Royal Family, and a multitude of celebrities have spoken out about the problems of mental illness, reducing stigma, and encouraging treatment. Additionally, individual brave souls are sharing their experiences online through social media every day.

What can you do? Spread the work about your recovery, one person at a time. As a psychiatrist, I try to correct inaccurate words or phrases when I hear them. If I hear another medical professional referring to a "schizophrenic," I will inform them that it is more correct to refer to a "person with schizophrenia, just as a person with diabetes is not a 'diabetic'." This was a hard one, even for me. I'm not perfect and this is something I have to keep working on. But it is one example of how we can all have an impact on reducing stigma; sharing, communicating, and educating others.

Start by correcting your own thoughts and phrases. Avoid loaded and negative words and instead select empowering words. Use these improved words and phrases with your medical and mental health practitioners. Once you have this new awareness, you may find yourself politely educating others.

Today, stigma regarding mental illness is lower than it has ever been in the history of the United States and the world. The U.S. government has passed the Mental Health Parity Act that requires medical insurance companies to cover mental health treatment. Every major VA hospital has a Local Recovery Coordinator, whose sole job is to educate veterans and health care providers about mental health recovery. We have biological medications, psychological therapies, and social interventions to help treat mental health. Additionally, with the vast amount of research, and easy access to books and internet. We have reason to be hopeful!

The 21ˢᵗ Century Mental Health Crisis

There is a crisis in mental health treatment. According to one study, the United States is in need of 45,000 psychiatrists. Most (75%) counties in America have a "severe shortage" of psychiatrists and nearly all (96%) of the counties have "some shortage" of psychiatrists.[15] These statistics are concerning to me, as I have seen this shortage first hand. I have worked across the country during my training and practice of psychiatry. Even when working in areas with a large number of psychiatrists, I have encountered outpatient wait times of over 3 months. This makes for a colossal barrier for those seeking treatment. If you do have a regular outpatient psychiatrist, count your blessings, as most are going without care.

Another impetus for educating others about social recovery is to empower those lacking standard mental health care, at least until you can get in with a provider. There are important reasons to include appropriate medical and psychiatric providers, namely appropriate diagnosis and treatment. Correct diagnosis includes evaluating for underlying causes, including important medical causes. For example, one of the most common medical causes of depressive symptoms is hypothyroidism, which requires treating the underlying glandular condition.

Unparalleled Hope for the Future of Mental Health Treatment

Luckily for us all, we have the right to humane treatment. We have the ability to incorporate medications, talk therapy, and social interventions into your recovery. Because of this personalized approach to mental health treatment, I believe there has never been a better time in the history of the world to be diagnosed with a psychological condition!

Chapter 5:

Introduction to Mental Health Recovery

The Next Frontier of Mental Health Treatment

I want to introduce a topic which may be the single most important idea for anyone affected by any form of mental distress or psychiatric diagnosis: the concept of social recovery.

To help us understand recovery, we begin by looking at some basic recovery fundamentals.

The study of mental health recovery is termed psychosocial rehabilitation. Psychosocial rehabilitation is defined by services and interventions that have been studied by rigorous scientific methods that have demonstrated significant effectiveness in treating severe mental illness.

Recovery is called different names by different people. *I use the terms social recovery, personal recovery, mental health recovery, and recovery interchangeably.*

The term recovery means different things to different people, and there are actually several different definitions. I'll use the one referenced by the Substance Abuse and Mental Health Services Administration (SAMHSA), "a process of change through which individuals improve their health and wellness, live a self-directed life, and strive to reach their full potential."[16]

Another definition is "the concept of recovery refers to a person diagnosed with a serious mental illness reclaiming his or her right to a safe, dignified, and personally meaningful and gratifying life in the community despite his or her psychiatric condition."

Yet another is "a deeply personal, unique process of changing one's attitudes, values, feelings, goals, skills and/or roles...a way of living a satisfying, hopeful and contributing life even with the limitations caused by illness."[17]

That's great, but how does that translate into something tangible? It proposes that an individual doesn't have to wait until the psychological stress is completely eliminated before beginning their journey into recovery. I have heard mental illness called "the invisible illness" because you can't "see" the mental injury. To better understand this concept let's compare mental health recovery to a medical form of recovery from a physical injury, like a broken bone, to see what I mean about not waiting to start your recovery.

When recovering from a bone fracture, you don't lie in bed for weeks or months until the bone is healed. Bones are aligned and then immobilized; the body immediately begins the healing process on a cellular level.

Within days, physical therapists are pushing you to your physical limits, assisting with stretching, strengthening and using devices such as wheelchairs, walkers, and crutches. A person then gradually increases his or her activity until he or she eventually reaches a full level of functioning.

In depression, people tend to take a much less active role in immediate recovery, but it is just as necessary, even when the ability to function can be painfully exhausting. If they don't, I have seen people completely engulfed in isolation for decades - a most devastating result.

Waiting for your mental stress symptoms to go away before resuming regular daily and work tasks is like saying that you have to lie in bed for 6 weeks while your broken bone heals. You know that isn't practical, as you would lose muscle mass by not using your body regularly. Complete immobility with a healing fracture would be detrimental to your health, so too with avoiding regular daily tasks and activities while healing from mental stress.

Therefore, I give you my definition of recovery: *Living your life to the fullest in spite of mental disorders and symptoms.*

Recovery is so important because it directly addresses the underlying functioning that every mental illness disrupts. I believe that it *is the defining tool and the next frontier of mental health treatment.* Unfortunately, I believe that it is an underutilized treatment even though the only barrier to its use is a lack of awareness and implementation.

Recovery sounds like a simple thing. But after years of study and over a decade of clinical experience, it turns out that recovery is one of the most complicated things to achieve, even with help from a mental health specialist. The first time I heard the term recovery was during my psychiatric training. It was used in the discussion related to recovery from alcohol and other drug addictions. I use the term much more broadly; to me, recovery not only relates to addiction, but to all forms of mental illness. Serious mental illnesses include not only schizophrenia, but also bipolar disorder, major depression and anxiety disorders. Each of these conditions have shown ongoing dysfunction and disability even when symptom remission has been achieved.[18] Knowing this, I believe that social recovery treatments are the best interventions that target these disabilities. I want everyone who is struggling with mental illness to be in mental health recovery.

Introduction to Dr. Paul Rashid's 10 Elements of Recovery

You may be thinking, okay Dr. Paul, so what is this social therapy? Social therapy was the impetus for writing this book. I found myself learning about social recovery, yet I was unable to find any good sources for patient education. Sure, I was reading volumes of scientific research, but there was nothing easily digestible for those without a medical or psychological background. Even within the research, there were minor differences between definitions and interventions. In my group discussions with clients I found myself struggling to communicate this method. I believe that it should not be difficult to relay this life changing information, it should be easy. I reviewed the research and distilled recovery into the 10 basic elements consistently referenced and utilized by recovering individuals. The elements are not meant to be prescriptive; I am not saying that you must incorporate all 10 elements into your life. But these 10 elements have been consistently beneficial for those that are in recovery. Some may resonate with you, some may not, but the more you are able to incorporate, the more robust your recovery will be. I believe these 10 social domains are bridges that aid in the recovery process. I have listed the 10 elements and each will be discussed in detail in their corresponding chapters in Part III.

1. Awareness – Recovery demands honesty, consciousness, and an openness to other perspectives.

2. Home Environment – We all need a safe place to reside.

3. Physical Health – Power your recovery with a nutritious diet and good physical health.

4. Purpose – What are your daily drives? Realize them and rediscover your recovery path.

5. Community – Your community is based on where you live and with whom you interact.

6. Non-Linear – Problems come and go, as with all journeys. Recovery is no different.

7. Hope – Recovery is real. People can and do recover from their challenges and obstacles.

8. Personal Responsibility – Although you may have help along the way, you are accountable for your recovery.

9. Self-Determination – Your recovery is as unique and individualized as you are; you shape your recovery.

10. Spirituality – Your spiritual beliefs play an important role in recovery.

Living in Spite of Symptoms

Recovery makes me think about the biological term, homeostasis, defined by biology-online.org as "The ability of the body or a cell to seek and maintain a condition of equilibrium or stability within its internal environment when dealing with external changes."

Nothing in this world is static; nothing is fixed or permanent. It is very easy to buy into the default belief that everything appears exactly as it is, but it is not. We are composed of atoms that are in a constant state of movement and vibration.

Our bodies are always in a state of flux, and through homeostasis, the body is continuously striving to maintain an optimal healthy living balance. Your skin cells are constantly growing and dividing into new cells while shedding dead ones. Your bones are constantly being broken down and rebuilt, your liver is in a constant state of regeneration, and every day, red blood cells are being degraded and recycled, and new red blood cells are created in your bone marrow. There are examples for every organ and system in your body.

What does this have to do with psychiatry, mental health, or recovery? My point is that we are all in recovery from the moment we are born - physically, mentally, and spiritually.

From the time we are born and take our first breath, or when we are grieving the loss of a loved one, or trying to figure out our place in the cosmos, we are in a constant flux of homeostasis and recovery. We are seeking stability within our minds while dealing with difficult life events. The only difference between our minds and bodies is that our bodies maintain homeostasis without any effort, but our minds require active effort to remain in balance. That effort may be in the form of meditation, learning how to halt negative thoughts, a new learning endeavor, or some other mental engagement, but it does require some form of action, none the less.

So recovery is really "the process and journey of life in spite of what obstacles that are thrown in your way." It is when we forget that life is in continuous motion that we become distressed. Once you accept this concept that anyone alive is in recovery, you will have made a significant mental shift. You will find yourself in a place where healing can begin and take root.

When my clients add social recovery to their current treatment, a transformation occurs. They improve faster. Moods improve and sustain. They become more active and engage in activities that were long neglected. They find renewed purpose. They pursue their work or educational goals. Their relationships with their spouses, children, and friends improve. This is why I say that recovery is the future of mental health treatment.

"In Recovery" verses "Recovered From"

Is there a difference between "Recovery From" and being "In Recovery?" Recovery can be a difficult concept to understand. So let's clear up a minor, but important point. *When I use the terms recovery, social recovery, personal recovery, or mental health recovery, I am referring to the same concept.*

Recovery is about living a functional and full life. One question I am often asked is whether a person can recover from mental conditions. *Yes and No.* Remember, there is no cure for any mental illness. I conceptualize this in the recovery model as follows: there is no "cure" for the ups and downs of life. For example, saying that you are "recovered from depression" is inaccurate because we know that if there has been one episode, there is a high probability that there will be future episodes. This example applies to all mental disorders ranging from anxiety to schizophrenia. Yes, there are periods of improvement, but very commonly there may be ongoing residual symptoms. Therefore, there is no "recovery from" illness, as the underlying condition doesn't cease to exist, but, you can be living "in recovery," whether symptoms are present or not.

"Being in recovery" adds another level to the process and better captures its active nature. It takes a person out of passive treatment and into active management so that one may heal. After all, this is your life and your recovery; you need to take an active part in it despite any ongoing psychiatric symptoms. That is definitely possible for everyone.

Saying that you are "in recovery" is a small change in wording and what a difference this can make, not only in your mind, but also in the minds of others, when discussing recovery. Use it when thinking about your recovery and say it when talking about your recovery with friends, family, and mental health providers.

Chapter 6:

The Bio-Psycho-Social Formulation

How do physicians assess the myriad of complex factors affecting physical and mental health? Dr. Gregory Engel, an American psychiatrist, created an approach to do just that in 1977; the bio-psycho-social formulation. It was designed to capture and organize physical, emotional, and environmental factors that impact health.

The Three domains are as follows:

1. Bio from Biology - These are the genetic factors specific to your personal biology and physiology. This encompasses genetics, nutrition, medical conditions, medications, chemical exposure, and exercise.

2. Psych from Psychological - Relating to your psychological makeup, your thoughts, emotions, and behaviors. Your personal psychology includes your beliefs and coping mechanisms which affect your view and perception of the world.

3. Social from, well, social - All external interactions define social interactions including factors of environment, religion, relationships, culture, and your individual background and life experiences.

How the Bio-Psycho-Social Formulation Works

This formulation is regularly used by mental health care professionals including psychiatrists, psychologists, social workers, and other talk therapists. It is created after reviewing a person's medical, psychological, developmental, and environmental histories. This allows providers to make sense out of very complex information. A treatment plan is then created to address the client's underlying strengths and deficits.

Each element is divided into strengths and weakness. Identifying strengths allows one to identify what is already working and continue to utilize such skills. Recognizing weakness enables one to hone in on barriers and come up with plans to navigate future struggles. Both strengths and weaknesses can then be applied to each person's unique mental health treatment.

An Example of the Biopsychosocial Formulation

Let's review a simplified case to see how this works. You might read a Biopsychosocial formulation at the end of a psychiatric assessment that sounds something like this:

"Mrs. Anderson is a 30-year-old female complaining of depression with symptoms of difficulty initiating sleep, low energy, poor concentration, and low appetite. Biologically, she has medical conditions of obesity and diabetes which are treated with the medication Metformin. She exercises 3 days a week, eats fast food during the work week, but has more control on the weekends when she cooks at home. Psychologically, she reports first experiencing emotional problems when her parents divorced when she was 10 years old. She copes with stress by smoking. She feels guilty about yelling at co-workers and family members, and also reports relationship trust issues. Socially, she has been isolating herself from social events with friends due to lower energy levels. Although she identifies with being Christian, she no longer participates in religious services or prayer."

The physician would then sub-divide each bio-psycho-social domain into strengths and weaknesses. The physician would then prescribe continued use of the client's strengths, while giving additional treatments to address their deficits. The treatment plan may look like this:

"Biologically, Mrs. Anderson should optimize her diabetes and blood glucose control to prevent blood sugar induced mood swings and irritability. Areas to address include obesity, diet, and nutrition. She is already cooking at home on weekends, and could find ways to cook healthy meals with increasing frequency at home. Psychologically, Mrs. Anderson has poor frustration tolerance and coping skills. Interventions may be anger management, relaxation therapy, or coping skills training. Once she has greater ability controlling anger and irritability, consider smoking cessation that will improve her physical health. She may have relationship issues related to her parents' divorce which are having an impact on her current work and family relationships which psychotherapy will address when she is ready for a referral. Socially, she is less engaged with friends, and I would encourage her to participate in spite of feeling less energetic. Lastly, she has not been spiritually engaged, despite her upbringing. We should consider discussions about prayer and church related participation."

I hope this simple case illustrates the biopsychosocial formulation and the way it is utilized to identify strengths and weaknesses with subsequent interventions. Please note, patient education is a substantial portion of this in regards to: medications, diet, lifestyle, psychological education, and discussion regarding patient's beliefs and preferences. Additionally, these interventions may take several appointments to address and follow up. The treatment plan also changes and adapts based on the evolving symptoms, environmental stressors and additional variables.

Common Bio-Psycho-Social Interventions

   A. Biological Interventions

Medications are the most common biologic treatments. Most people are familiar with the medical model where a physician or psychiatrist will prescribe a medication to treat an underlying illness or symptom. I do believe that there's a place for medications. There are effective treatments for many people struggling with anxiety, mood, or psychotic disorders.

In fact, I feel medication is even more important for someone just starting in the recovery process. I sometimes conceptualize medication as a way to tone down stress or "lengthen your fuse." This allows you to better cope while dealing with daily stressors. For example, you may have a personal educational recovery goal of enrolling in a class. As we all know from early endeavors in elementary and high school, learning environments carry with them potentially stressful situations such as interacting with new people, being in crowds, learning course material, and test taking issues. This can cause anxiety for many. Individuals may benefit from medications in this case, maximizing their academic achievement and stress management.

B. Psychological Interventions

Psychological theories have been around for centuries and have been useful tools to allow persons to get in touch with the deepest part of their psyche and better understand their thoughts, feelings, and behaviors.

Psychoanalysis was founded in the 1890's by the famous Austrian psychiatrist and neurologist Sigmund Freud. It has been helpful for some, but there are many barriers to this form of treatment such as the daily, hour-long appointments that last for years, and it is quite costly. Additionally, over the last century, there have been countless psychological theories, frameworks, and schools of thought. The difficult question then becomes, "which one to choose?"

Luckily, psychologists have developed a variety of psychotherapies. One technique has repeatedly stood out for its consistent and reproducible benefit, Cognitive Behavioral Therapy (CBT). CBT focuses on the relationship between beliefs, emotions, and actions. CBT is relatively short in duration compared to other therapies, quite cost-effective, and usually covered by health insurance. CBT typically consists of one-hour sessions, once a week, for approximately 12 weeks. The basic principal of CBT is to uncover and change disabling beliefs. The new, empowering thoughts cause a chain reaction in our behaviors and emotions. Unfortunately, CBT is restricted by the limited number of trained therapists and few referrals.

C. Social Interventions

The third and final domain of the bio-psycho-social formulation is social. By definition, diagnosing any psychiatric or psychological condition requires impairment in either social, occupational or scholastic functioning. Just as we spoke about a broken bone requiring "physical rehab," think of social recovery as a "social rehab" for psychological conditions. My 10 elements of recovery are the different kinds of "social rehab." Think of these as social interventions for mental and social difficulties. They are the basis of mental health recovery, also called social recovery or simply recovery. The elements have shown benefits for others. Think of each element as a way to guide your focus. These are things that make up your social self and can provide specific interventions to improve your mental health. You can choose how you approach your social interventions; they are controlled and directed by you alone. You may choose to include others to assist in the process, such as your mental health provider or friends and family, for suggestions and feedback. We explore each element of recovery in detail in Part III of this book.

Most people aren't aware of, or even offered, social interventions. These are not only underutilized interventions; *they're not even on the map.* This is also the area where *you have the ability to exert the most control.*

Most persons receiving mental health treatment typically receive only one treatment modality--usually medication, sometimes psychotherapy, and rarely social recovery. Each area has research evidence showing improvement in mental health symptoms and overall functioning. We know a single intervention with either medication, psychology, or social domain is effective. Imagine the response you could experience by stacking two or three of these treatments on top of each other!

Chapter 7:

The Evidence for Social Recovery in Schizophrenia

The PORT Study

The National Institute of Mental Health (NIMH) is one of the major federally-funded research groups in the United States. It funded a landmark review of evidenced-based treatment for schizophrenia, named The Patient Outcomes Research Team, or the PORT study for short. It was first published in 1998 with a subsequent revision in 2008.[19] The goal was simple: improve the quality of care given to those with schizophrenia. Schizophrenia can include some of the most debilitating symptoms of mental illness. Many treatments have attempted to provide relief from these symptoms over the centuries and this study allowed psychiatrists to use only treatments that have the strongest evidence.

As one may imagine, medications were the most reviewed. Thankfully, we have effective medications for this disorder. But my favorite section in the PORT study isn't about the 16 medications found to be effective. What I like best are the eight psychosocial, non-pharmacological treatments that have been found to be effective for schizophrenia and other psychotic illnesses.

The eight effective psychosocial interventions include: Assertive Community Treatment (ACT), Supported Employment, Skills Training, Cognitive Behavioral Therapy (CBT), Token Economy, Family-Based Services, Substance Treatment, and Weight Management.

I will organize these based on my 10 Elements of Recovery:

- Element #4 – Purpose (Work and Education): Supported Employment, Skills Training, and Token Economy.

- Element #5 - Community (Support Network): Assertive Community Treatment (ACT) and Family-Based Services.
- Element #6 - Physical Health: Substance Treatment and Weight Management.
- Psychological (Not under my 10 elements, but part of the psychological treatments found in the Bio-Psycho-Social Formulation): Cognitive Behavior Therapy (CBT).

Here is a brief description of each of these effective treatments.

- Assertive Community Treatment (ACT) is a very good support program with great "wrap around" services that usually includes a case manager with very frequent contact, a prescriber and a nurse. The most common diagnosis for persons receiving ACT services is Schizophrenia, but anyone that has had repeated psychiatric hospitalizations or homelessness may be considered. ACT has been shown to reduce hospitalization and homelessness.

- Supported employment is an effective resource for those with psychological symptoms that require assistance to achieve their goal of meaningful work.

- Skills training is provided in a group therapy setting and can help those seeking improvement in their socialization by bolstering social aptitude.

- Token Economy is a system typically used in hospitalization or residential care that provides positive reinforcement for personal hygiene and healthy social interaction.

- Family-based services are interventions geared towards family illness education, crisis intervention, emotional support, and training about how to cope with illness and related problems. This usually lasts between 6 and 9 months. This has been shown to reduce the relapse rate of illness and re-hospitalization.

- Alcohol and substance use disorder interventions are effective for all persons suffering from mental disorders. This is sometimes referred to as "Dual Diagnosis," because treating providers are treating both mental health and addiction issues.

- Psychosocial interventions for weight management are comprised of education on nutrition, caloric intake and expenditure, portion control, and behavioral self-management.

I believe the important take-away from this study as regarding schizophrenia and all mental illnesses include:

- Multiple pharmacological treatments exist.
- We have eight psychosocial interventions that have been found to be very effective.
- All of the above-mentioned evidence based psychosocial treatments match up with the Elements of Recovery.

Social interventions are found to be effective for some of the most difficult chronic mental illness symptoms, *so why aren't we using these social interventions for the treatment of all mental health disorders?*

Chapter 8:

Personal Preference and Spirituality

What's the Point?

A common existential question pondered throughout the millennia is "What is the meaning of life?" I spent much thought on this question in my early adulthood. I have concluded, from both my personal experiences and from spiritual discovery, that our gift of life is really a gift of experiences. We have been placed on this beautiful and amazing earth so that we may enjoy the bliss of life in all its richness and beauty. I mention my personal views here, only because this ties back into the social recovery model of preference.

Sometimes when things are not going well, we resort to short-term, quick solutions that we know will work. We find ourselves repeating the same behaviors and choices. If we are feeling depressed, for example, we may not feel like joining friends for an activity so we choose to stay home. This isolation may feel beneficial in the moment but has long-term detrimental consequences. After months and years of this behavior and you finally wake up one day and realize the crippling effect of this pattern. In this state of isolation there may be a feeling of emptiness which gets back to my original thesis: the point of life is to have purposeful and meaningful experiences.

Rediscovery and Adventure

Recovery is all about looking at the world through a child's eyes, trying new and exciting experiences. It's how you discovered your favorite game, sport, food, music - the list goes on and on. But over time, we tend to make fewer and fewer new choices and can end up finding ourselves making the same, stale choice over and over. The recovery process is about going back to the drawing board and trying something different. You may find that you identify a new favorite activity.

Rediscovering pleasurable activities and regularly engaging in those that bring us and others joy can help in recovery.

Take for example trying to figure out what to order at a restaurant. We've all had the dilemma of picking our favorite dish versus trying something new. The benefit of ordering a known dish is getting something familiar which will leave you satisfied. The risk of being adventurous with your dinner selection is the possibility that you may not like this new option. But the potential payoff is that you find something you enjoy even more than your previous "safe" entrée. I'm thankful for the times I have stepped outside of my comfort zone because I have found some of my favorite foods and activities as a result.

Now let's relate this back to recovery. The cool thing about recovery is you get to pick and choose what you incorporate. Some people prefer to select a medication intervention with their physician, even if temporarily, others prefer no medication at first. Some people wish to include talk therapy. Your preference options become vast once you delve into the social interventions. As you learn about the 10 Elements of Recovery, make a conscious effort to select what you wish to include in your plan.

Mind, Body, and Spirit

We're not just creatures of flesh and blood. We are spiritual beings having a physical experience in the physical body of flesh and blood. I liken it to a car and driver metaphor: the vehicle is our body and the driver is our spirit. I believe that most people have some sense of this, but in varying degrees. Some people believe we are connected to a higher energy, call it God, spirit, soul, or universal oneness. Most major religions have a belief in a higher energy or power - something greater than the individual. They also share a fundamental belief that all people are linked to this higher power or oneness. The degree to which we are linked varies from person to person but are linked, all the same. American psychologist Abraham Maslow created the human Hierarchy of Needs. In Maslow's hierarchy, self-actualization is the highest level of psychological development and consciousness. This occurs when an individual has an awareness shift or epiphany that he is the same as everyone else. Many times there is an understanding that we all originally came into this world from a similar origin. We are in fact, only different from one another by the individual preferences we have developed in the short time of our physical existence.

Joseph Campbell, an American mythologist, studied ancient man's myths from around the world and came up with this beautiful quote "follow your bliss." Life is joyous and when you are doing what you were set out to do in this life--following your bliss--your life will be more joyous and prosperous.

Chapter 9:

Socialization

Does Socialization Really Matter?

One difficulty I had when learning about social recovery was comprehending the impact socialization has on a person. I thought, "Sure, socializing is fun, but that's where the benefits end, right?" Wrong.

Researchers have looked at how the method of socialization and number of social contacts impacted the level of depression in older adults over a two-year period. The conclusion was clear that persons with in-person contact were less depressed; in addition, those that had more frequent social contact were less depressed.[20]

Socialization is the Heart of Mental Health

Social isolation and death. Yeah, you read that correctly. Death! I remember coming across a landmark study very clearly. This study measured the difference between individuals with an adequate to high-level of social relationships with family members, co-workers, friends, and neighbors to those that had few relationships. They discovered that socially active people were 50% more likely to survive the study compared to those with reduced socialization.[21] Socialization is at the heart of mental health. Socialization is not just something warm and fuzzy. It is essential for a long and healthy life.

Socialization and Culture

We are social beings through and through. We are completely dependent on our parents during infancy. The family unit is based on the social interaction between relatives. Even today, people in many countries continue to live with three, and sometimes four generations, in one household. The roots of society began as branches of family trees. Small family tribes grew to create towns and villages.

Significant aspects of our culture have developed due to socialization including language, customs, beliefs, rituals, values, work, recreation, and even how and what we eat. After thinking about this, it makes complete sense that the rate of depression would increase as the frequency and quality of our social contact diminishes.

I believe that the advancing technological world, although full of amazing benefits, has cut out much of our social contact. In the fast-paced western society, we hurry to work and hurry to "run" errands. We miss out on our children's sports games and recitals. Three and four generations of family members rarely live in the same city or state, let alone under the same roof. We miss out on the transmission of culture, history, and the knowledge of our forefathers. Many times we get distracted with television and the internet, often neglecting meaningful social interaction. Increasingly, "quality time" is being substituted with some abstract version of this in which family members, if even in the same room, are focused on television, electronic devices, or other individual tasks. Is that quality time?

Relationships Matter

The key point to remember is that all of our relationships matter. Our family, friends, co-workers, and social interactions within our community are vital. They matter to the deepest fabric of our genetic makeup. They impact our physical and emotional health.

Based on the scientific evidence above, you might even say that socializing is a "vitamin" for optimal health. I conceptualize this idea as follows: when we are disconnected from that purpose, we plummet into a state of anxiety and despair. At times we may become obsessed with our own inner turmoil and focus on our fears. *The trick to stop this inner turmoil is to reconnect with others.* This helps us rediscover that inner balance and bliss. So, remember to take your "Social Vitamin."

Chapter 10:

Empowerment and Utilizing Strengths

"The most important decision we make is whether we believe we live in a friendly or hostile universe" – Albert Einstein

Empowerment

Julian Rotter, an American psychologist, developed a Social-Learning Theory of Personality called Locus of Control in 1954. This is a powerful psychological concept in which individuals perceive the amount of control they have over their life events. Persons with an external locus of control tend to perceive outside events as beyond their control. Whereas individuals with an internal locus of control believe they have significant influence on the outcome of life events. One study found that older adults who demonstrated a strong sense of personal control over their quality of life and physical health were more resilient and experienced improved health outcomes.[22] The more you utilize the internal locus of control mentality, the more empowered you and your recovery will become.

Social recovery is about *empowering you to make a difference in your life.* The buck stops with you. You are the most influential person you know; you just need to rediscover your power. I believe we have outsourced our power. We have outsourced our individual and collective power to governments, which has resulted in a gamut of educational, health, and financial crises. We have outsourced our health to the health care system, industrial complexes, and fast food. This results in the blind and uninformed acceptance of unhealthy practices. It is mushrooming into a healthcare crisis with epidemics of diabetes and obesity. This is happening in the most technologically-advanced societies, not to mention the developing nations, which are the fastest implementers of wireless technology.

We need to advocate for ourselves. No one cares more about your health than you. No one cares more about how you feel than you. Family, friends, physicians, and talk therapist may care and want the best for you, but you must be the one leading the way. You are steering your way through life. You have a choice. You can either be passive and outsource your mental health or you can choose empowerment by reclaiming your post as the captain of your recovery.

Education is one way to reclaim this power. You are educating yourself right now by reading this book and learning about mental health, commonly referred to as "psychoeducation." Research has found that something as simple and non-invasive as psychoeducation can reduce symptoms relapse, readmission rates, and length of psychiatric hospitalizations in those diagnosed with schizophrenia.[23] One study found that hospital readmission rates were 64% higher for those that did not receive illness education.[24] Learning is the way to upgrade yourself, and the information in this book is going to upgrade your psychoeducation to version 2.0!

What kind of impact would we all have if we made conscious decisions about every dollar we spent? Take for instance, one of my passions, healthy food selection. I choose to spend my hard-earned money on organic and unprocessed foods. I choose to vote with my dollar, and as a result, the food industry hears this message loud and clear. I have gone from someone who didn't even know what the term organic meant in 2010, to now finding organic foods the same price as, and at times, even cheaper than the chemically-laden industrial versions. An increasing percentage of the population is doing this and large food corporations are listening and producing more organic foods.

Take responsibility for your health. It may feel burdensome, but this is the only life you get, please don't squander it. You are already on your way by reading this book. Educate yourself about your medical illnesses and invite your doctors into this conversation so that you can make comprehensively informed decisions.

Utilizing Strengths

Learning about recovery and implementing new habits into your life can feel overwhelming. It doesn't have to be, though. You can start with your natural skills and talents. When you begin with the elements you are already effectively using, you have bypassed the learning curve. Utilization of a strength based approach improves outcomes including lower hospitalization rates, better employment/education attainment, and interpersonal outcomes such as self-efficacy and a sense of hope.[25]

Not sure what your strengths are? That's alright. Some things may resonate with you as you read through my 10 elements of recovery. For example, let us say the spirituality and religious chapter strikes you. You are already established with a place of worship. Build on that social intervention. Maybe you're just going to a weekly service. Think bigger; make it a point to participate in programs through that organization. Maybe there is a social night, or a voluntary effort, go ahead and join in.

This goes for coping skills as well. You may already have your favorite relaxation method. You may paint, listen to music, or maybe you prefer to go for a walk or exercise. Keep doing what naturally works for you. Sometimes the things in life that come easiest are the most beneficial. You may apply this approach to each component of recovery. Pursue your strengths and your recovery will follow, but do not ignore new skills or elements of recovery either. Yes, learning a new process takes time to practice and master, but can have substantial pay offs. For instance, deep breathing is a very powerful calming exercise. For deep breathing to be effective in a panic state, it must be repeatedly practiced in a calm state. Remember that new skill you're working on may one day be your future strength. Make it a priority to know your strengths and use them often.

PART II

The Wheel of Recovery

Chapter 11:

Dr. Paul Rashid's Wheel of Recovery

Mental disorders are severely debilitating and it is difficult to navigate these issues on your own. It is very common to observe social withdrawal and physical isolation in depressive and anxiety disorders, PTSD, schizophrenia, and schizoaffective disorders. Sometimes social withdrawal has progressed for so many years, that people have difficulty reengaging in previous social activities. Attempts to jump back into past social activities may be met with severe anxiety and panic symptoms. The Wheel of Recovery is like the blueprint for healthy social interactions and functioning. Healthy social interactions can fuel our recovery. Many times mental stress has caused us to descend to our depths—and we need a guide to show us the way out.

Ideally, you would include all or most of the components of recovery to some degree in your life. I like to compare recovery to a bicycle wheel in my "wheel of recovery" concept. Each domain of recovery is like a spoke in the wheel. A bicycle wheel that is missing one or two spokes will probably get you from point A to B, but missing too many spokes and your bike will break down and collapse from the lack of support. If your social recovery is deficient in multiple components, it may not be as robust or as effective. The majority of your wheel should have activity in most or all components. Each element is explained in detail in Part III.

Dr. Paul Rashid's Wheel of Recovery

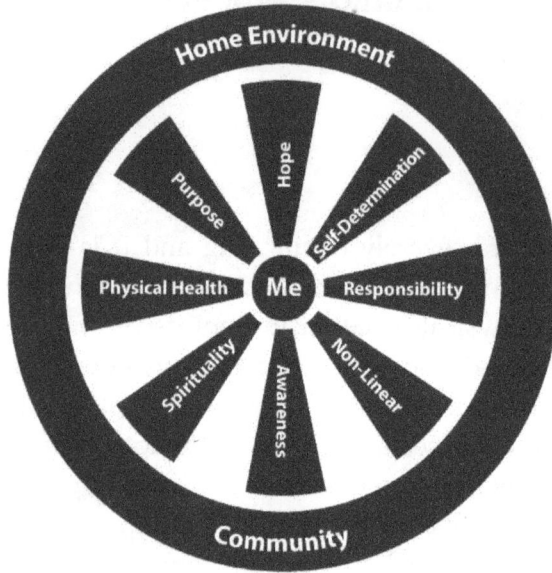

1. Awareness – Recovery demands honesty, consciousness, and an openness to other perspectives.

2. Home Environment – We all need a safe place to reside.

3. Physical Health – Power your recovery with a nutritious diet and good physical health.

4. Purpose – What are your daily drives? Realize them and rediscover your recovery path.

5. Community – Your community is based on where you live and with whom you interact.

6. Non-Linear – Problems come and go, as with all journeys. Recovery is no different.

7. Hope – Recovery is real. People can and do recover from their challenges and obstacles.

8. Personal Responsibility – Although you may have help along the way, you are accountable for your recovery.

9. Self-Determination – Your recovery is as unique and individualized as you are; you shape your recovery.

10. Spirituality – Your spiritual beliefs play an important role in recovery.

Recovery Questions:

1. What does your Wheel of Recovery look like now?

2. What would you like your wheel of recovery to look like in three months, six months, and one year?

The Black and White Wheel of Recovery is great, but my color version is even better! I recommend printing it out and posting it where you will pass by it as a daily reminder. Feel free to share it with friends, family, and your doctors and mental health providers. Download your free copy at PaulRashidMD.com or scan the QR code below.

Part III

The 10 Components of Recovery

Chapter 12:

Element #1 - Awareness

Definition: Awareness – noun - the state or condition of being aware; having knowledge; consciousness

Awareness: A Prerequisite for Recovery

By definition, recovery is an active process of change; if one is not aware they will not be able to change. There is a term called "alexithymia" which is when a person has difficulty naming the emotions they are feeling. Those with alexithymia tend to have higher rates of both anxiety and depression.[26] Behavioral Therapy, which also increases awareness, is an effective treatment for anxiety and depression.[27] Therefore, you must be conscious of areas of dysfunction in your life or at least aware of your hopes, dreams, or desires to make the changes for a brighter future. You must know what you are dealing with so that you may create a recovery plan and execute it.

It's pretty hard to overcome an obstacle if you don't know that it's present. For instance, a track and field athlete must train and come up with a strategy to safely jump hurdles. Otherwise he or she suffers the consequences of hitting a hurdle obstacle and enduring injury, pain, and further suffering. Likewise, you must beware of and identify your obstacle and how it is impairing you. It wasn't difficult for me; it's pretty hard to ignore a full-blown panic attack. No one had to tell me that I was spiraling out of control when I slumped down on the convention center floor. Anxiety isn't very hard to identify. But some symptoms are more difficult to identify than others. Disorders of mood and thought may be difficult to detect and a psychiatric evaluation may be beneficial.

Awareness is required for recovery. By definition, without awareness, you are unable to be in recovery. You will just be spinning out of control in denial. Denial will keep you from growing and will interfere with your ability to lead a happier and fulfilling life.

Know Thy Enemy

I needed to create a strategy to combat my adversary; anxiety. I researched symptoms, courses, causes, and treatments. I don't want you to spend all of your energy on the illness, but you have to know your obstacle before you can come up with a plan to defeat it. For without this awareness, you have no understanding or sense of direction. I'm not saying to dwell on the "disorder." I'm simply saying that education contributes to the awareness necessary for recovery.

Once you have an understanding of your obstacle, you can then create your strategy with the aid of mental health professionals, family, and friends so that you may begin your recovery. Recognizing your particular challenges will pull you out of a tailspin and keep you from repeatedly banging your head against the wall of symptoms. It will allow you to create your life with purpose and meaning so you may flourish.

An Example of Awareness in Recovery

Tom was diagnosed with bipolar disorder in his early 20's. He had multiple involuntary psychiatric hospitalizations for mania. Tom tended to overdo it, ignore his cycling mood disorder, and often adjusted medications on his own without informing his psychiatrist. At times he would feel good, too good, have less need for sleep, and begin working extended hours. His thinking would become distracted, and his family would notice him talking rapidly.

When I first met Tom, he had attempted suicide with an overdose of pills. He was feeling hopeless and tired of struggling with his illness of 30 years. I was able to work with Tom and introduce him to the topic of recovery. Together, we were able to discover his pattern of manic episodes. He was able to let go of blaming bipolar disorder, being passive, and he stopped being a victim. By increasing his consciousness about his illness, he was able to take control. He could stop concentrating on what he couldn't do and began focusing on his goals. His heightened awareness allowed him to switch from an external locus of control to an internal locus of control.

Levels of Awareness

There are numerous levels of awareness including physical, cognitive, emotional, spiritual, and external perspectives. You can work on developing each one.

Physical: One can be aware of one's own physical body; actions and movements in time and space. Where are you? What are you doing? Who and what is around you? Sometimes repetitive patterns of behaviors cause a person to be imprisoned in low levels of functioning and distress.

Cognitive: What are you thinking? Do you have automatic assumptions? Automatic thoughts are repetitive cognitive patterns that now occur without conscious thought and may result in worried or negative views.

Emotional: How am I feeling right now? Describe the feeling. How long will this feeling last? How long has it lasted in the past?

Spiritual: Are you mindful of daily religious or spiritual practices? Do you pray, have thoughts and feelings of gratitude, or have a connection with others or with nature during a walk?

Omniscient: Omniscient means "all knowing." Have you ever imagined seeing yourself from someone else's perspective? Having an outside attentiveness to one's self can be very powerful. Imagine that there is a video camera that is seeing everything that is occurring. "Watch" the camera footage as an outside observer. Remove your emotions from "film." Describe what is occurring to everyone involved, from each person's perspective and not just your own. Just like watching a movie, you may find yourself able to see the narrative from multiple perspectives. Taking a step outside of your own perspective can help you distance yourself and enable you to have a more balanced assessment of the situation.

Emotional Awareness Exercise. As you go about your day and experience negative emotions, answer these 3 questions:

1. What emotion am I feeling?
2. Where in my body am I feeling it?
3. How will I let go of this negative emotion?

Questions to improve your awareness:

1. Do you believe you are suffering from a mental disorder?
2. Have you ever been diagnosed with a mental disorder by a psychiatrist or physician?
3. Do symptoms interfere with your ability to complete daily activities? If yes, how so?
4. What difficulties are you having in school, work, or relationships?
5. Are you using drugs or alcohol to cope with stress? If yes, what do you believe it helps with?
6. Do drugs or alcohol impair your functioning? If yes, specify each problem substances cause.
7. How aware are you of your body, thoughts, feelings, and behaviors? What can you do to become more aware?
8. How would others perceive and describe you? How do you perceive and describe yourself?

Implementing Awareness:

1. Discuss psychiatric symptoms with your mental health practitioners.
2. If diagnosed with a disorder, educate yourself about it, ask your healthcare professional for resources.

3. Get feedback from others; ask trusted family and friends for feedback about how they perceive your functioning.
4. Make a list of problems that you would like to overcome.
5. Take some time and focus on your body, thoughts and emotions.
6. Imagine watching video footage of a recent stressful situation. Replay it from an outside perspective while removing your emotions. Look at it from everyone's point of view, not just your own. Just like watching a movie, you may find yourself able to see the narrative from multiple perspectives. Taking a step outside of your own perspective can help you distance yourself and enable you to have a more balanced assessment of the situation. What did you discover from this exercise?

Chapter 13:

Element #2 - Home Environment

Definition: Home - noun – any shelter, lodging, or dwelling place.

Physical Environment: Housing

Okay, so you have awareness of your situation, but without a safe residence, your efforts will be limited. We learned about Abraham Maslow's Hierarchy of Needs in Chapter 8. There we discussed the highest level of psychological development being self-actualization. Here I want to mention Maslow's basic human need, shelter. Regardless of which country or continent you live in, life is exceedingly difficult without the most basic needs of water, food, and safe shelter. Without these necessities, your thoughts and body will be in a state of stress and panic, as your very survival depends on acquiring these provisions moment to moment.

While working at a VA Hospital, I encountered Steve who was a veteran struggling with depression and hearing voices. I discovered a huge problem getting in the way of his recovery while completing his initial assessment. He was homeless. He had many valid reasons keeping him from attaining a stable residence. He was unable to secure temporary housing in a shelter, unable to reside with his ex-wife, and had very limited income. We worked together for many weeks, but he continued living in a wooded area in the city. I found myself becoming frustrated, not with Steve, but with my inability to assist him given his limited resources. Regardless of the best medication and talk therapy, how effective can anyone be in their recovery without a residence? A safe residence is required for recovery to take root. Homelessness, or residing with someone that is physically or emotional abusive, is going to halt your recovery in its tracks; it will probably cause worse stress and functioning. It can also make you vulnerable to further harm.

Just imagine recovering from a heart attack or broken leg. Would you be better off in a safe and protective home or exposed to the elements? I believe a scenario without housing would be significantly more challenging and may even cause thoughts of despair. But there is hope, and it makes the most sense to me that if you are homeless, your number one priority must be seeking stable housing. One study looked at persons with Type II sugar diabetes. They found that homelessness is a significant risk factor for uncontrolled blood glucose levels. This demonstrates the environmental limitations to physical recovery related to lack of housing.[28] Interventions addressing homelessness result in lower rates of mental illness symptoms and improvements in physical health.

Mental health is supported by having a regular schedule. If you are homeless, would you be sleeping well? Would you be taking your medications regularly? Would you be able to give your recovery 100%?

"Couch surfing" or crashing with friends is just as unstable. If you are homeless, make it your biggest priority to find housing. Couch surfing is even worse if you have alcohol or other addictions, as many times, the people you are staying with have the same unhealthy habits. This unstable combination tends to hold you back and push you further from recovery. Alternatively, finding a roommate with the same recovery goals may be very supportive; you can accelerate each other's recovery!

If you are homeless, you may want to start with a shelter. Homeless shelters have resources to help you work towards longer term stability. Consider staying with friends or family, but make this as temporary as possible as you work on your goal of securing shelter. You may qualify for subsidized housing. Local shelters have programs to assist with this process.

Many times I have worked with individuals that were getting behind on rent. Just the thought of eviction is enough to cause distress. Although scary, this is not a hopeless situation. If you find yourself in this situation, you have several options including saving money, working with friends and family, talking with your landlord, and looking into additional resources to catch up on your payments. You might want to consider paying rent in advance to avoid this from happening in the future.

Luckily, while I was working with Steve, we were able to work together, problem solve and he was ultimately able to find a half-way house that he could afford on his limited income. His ability to use coping exercises improved and his stress level decreased. He became engaged in his recovery after finding a safe residence. Make it your top priority and goal to find a residence. Housing is paramount for recovery.

Psychological Environment: Emotional Safety

The ability to feel calm and safe is important for both psychological and physical well-being. When we are exposed to unsafe environments we experience psychological stress. Mothers displaced by war report higher levels of psychological distress.[29] Psychological stress manifests in our bodies with the release of stress hormones. Cortisol, one such stress hormone, is known to weaken the immune system and interfere with the body's ability to heal. Cortisol can also cause elevated blood sugars in those with diabetes. We know that uncontrolled blood sugars can cause mood swings and irritability, further worsening psychiatric conditions.

When people perceive that they are living in safe neighborhoods, there is a significant association with psychological health.[30] One example of a safe micro-environment is during psychiatric and psychological appointments. I learned in my training that having a safe place to process difficult emotions aids, and actually leads to healing.

Ideally, your home environment is not only safe, but emotionally nurturing. How would it feel to not be stressed, but actually exist in an environment which fosters your functioning, creativity, self-expression, and joy?

Do you feel safe in your home environment? Are you a victim of physical, emotional, or verbal abuse? If physical abuse is occurring, each state has agencies for child and elderly abuse. If you are in an unhealthy relationship with any of the above issues, find your closest domestic shelter for resources and assistance.

Once you have a safe psychological environment, you will experience less stress. Your body will be able to function with greater ease. You will find more joy and happiness in your life. You will be in a better place to begin recovery.

Questions to assess your physical and emotional environment:

1. Is your current housing situation placing your physical and emotional well-being at risk? If so, describe.
2. Do you live in a safe place, with supportive individuals? If not, how could you improve the situation?

Housing Resources:

1. Local shelters may provide temporary housing as well as additional resources.
2. Consider a domestic shelter or state agency if abuse is present.
3. Discuss housing with friends, family, social workers or case managers.

Chapter 14:

Element #3 - Physical Health

Definition: Health - noun - the general condition of the body or mind with reference to soundness and vigor.

How do you treat your body? How is your physical health? What happens to your mood when you get a physical illness? I know that when I get a cold or flu, the smallest thing becomes difficult to accomplish. I also can get pretty cranky and irritable. This happens because illness causes inflammation and swelling. Inflammation is caused by the release of certain hormones. These hormones travel through our body and brain. Our brains are also sensitive to these hormone signals and may affect the way the brain processes emotions. Living with chronic illnesses such as diabetes and heart disease may have deleterious effects on our mood states. I conceptualize it like this; body illness lowers the brain's ability to function. In effect, this lowers your emotional threshold. So, now that you're compromised by, say the flu, you're more easily pushed into states of depression, anger, and anxiety.

If you want a better emotional state, you can start by improving your physical health. This is the mind-body connection, and science has demonstrated that you can't have one without the other. There is no quick fix either. I believe that we need to incorporate holistic treatment for our mind and body. An integral part should include a healthy diet as part of a healthy lifestyle. Nutritious food fuels our body and gives our cells the building blocks to replenish and repair themselves. Unfortunately the Standard American Diet is SAD; it's failing us and contributing to chronic medical and psychiatric illnesses. Are you feeding your body with healthy nutrients that will energize you or are you eating processed sludge that leaves you feeling sluggish and drained?

As a physician, I can only be as good as my ability to function. I learned early in my education that I must attend to my basic physical needs, so that I may be able to best help others. I pay particular attention to diet, sleep, exercise, and regular ongoing education.

One of the current theories of mental disorders including depression and anxiety is the "monoamine theory of illness." Monoamines are the neural chemical signals or neural transmitters in the brain and body that include serotonin, norepinephrine, and dopamine. This theory is based on the fact that antidepressants alter the amount of these chemicals in the brain. This is why some people say that mental disorders are "chemical imbalances." I believe nutrition is important, because these neurotransmitters enter your body from the food you ingest. Therefore, a diet rich in nutrients is imperative to ensure that your body has the raw materials, which the body converts to neurotransmitters, allowing your brain to work optimally and regulate these chemicals in the first place.

"Let food be thy medicine and medicine be thy food" is a quote attributed to the Greek physician Hippocrates, "The Father of Western Medicine" circa 400 BC.

My Approach to Basic Nutritional Concepts:

1. Whole Foods. Start with real, whole foods. This means whole vegetables and meats. Basically, your grandmother had it right, eat your veggies. Diets with high intake of vegetables, fish, and whole grains are associated with reduced risk of depression.[31] The Mediterranean Diet may prevent a multitude of brain diseases.[32] There have been robust findings that unhealthy diets are associated with worsening mental health in young people, as well as healthy diets having a protective effect on mood. This is encouraging for a whole diet approach to the prevention and treatment of mental illness.[33]

Let's take whole foods one step further. The "SMILES" trial (Supporting Modification of Lifestyle in Lower Emotional States) was a randomized controlled trial that studied dietary intervention in the treatment of moderate to severe depression. The two active controls compared healthy diet head-to-head with active supportive therapy. The nutritional intervention focused on diets higher in plant foods (vegetables, fruits, legumes, and whole grains) and lean meats such as fish, while limiting processed and sugary foods. The study had a real-world sampling of participants that continued on their current depression treatments. Most were prescribed antidepressants, many receiving both psychotherapy and medications, with a few only in psychotherapy. The participants were divided into two groups; the control group received a supportive therapy while the other group received the active dietary treatment. After 12 weeks, the dietary support group showed significant improvement in depression symptoms, as measured by a depression rating scale. As a nice bonus, they estimated food cost during the study. Amazingly, the dietary participant's average weekly food cost savings were over 20% when compared to their baseline diets before the study! If that wasn't enough, one in four people experienced remission in depression symptoms![34]

Why is this a big deal? To find out, let's compare it to this second study. Individuals who continued to experience depressive symptoms, despite being on antidepressant medications, were given a second antidepressant medication. In addition to added medication costs, the second, powerful antidepressant has multiple potential side effects. That study required 10 people to be treated for one person to experience remission of depression.[35]

Quick recap:

SMILES Study – Persons kept taking one antidepressant a day, but added healthy diet. *One out of every four* individuals achieved remission from depression.

Study 2 – Persons added a second daily antidepressant medication to the first. Only *one out of ten* persons experienced remission from depression.

This comparison reveals that dietary changes may exert robust improvements in mood, in this case about 2.5 times greater than prescribing an additional daily antidepressant medication for persons continuing to experience depression. This illustrates the potential impact that a healthy diet can have on improving severe depression.

The thought of cooking or preparing whole foods may be intimidating for some, but it doesn't have to be. You can actually make this process enjoyable. I like researching how to cook or prepare certain meals on YouTube. Many times it's simple because you are using whole foods that require only a few ingredients. Spice it up and make it interactive. Plan a cooking date in which the whole family or friends prepare dinner together; dine in, have fun, save money and get healthy!

2. Cut Down on Sugar and Processed Foods. Avoid highly processed foods; basically anything that comes in a box or bag. Unfortunately most minerals and vitamins are removed or destroyed during food processing. Additionally, many packaged foods have highly refined carbohydrates which become immediately converted to glucose in your body. This glucose spike, in the short term, can cause rapid mood shifts and irritability which then leads to carbohydrate craving, and the cycle then repeats itself. The long-term consequence of blood glucose spikes is diabetes. Diabetes is now an epidemic and has detrimental health effects on numerous body systems. A 2016 study revealed how the sugar industry sponsored and influenced medical studies in the 1960s and 70s. These articles downplayed sugar's harmful effects, while focusing on cholesterol and fat's role in deadly coronary heart disease.[36]

3. Ditch the Gluten. Flour and wheat food products contain gluten, as well as other plant proteins that can negatively affect our bodies, even if you do not have a "gluten celiac disease." Gluten-related disorders have been associated with major psychiatric disorders.[37] Even in those without celiac disease, gluten has been shown to increase gut permeability which may result in autoimmune dysfunction in areas of the brain.[38] Additionally, there is emerging data suggesting improvements in Attention Deficit Disorders and Schizophrenia when gluten is removed from the diet in certain people.[39,40] The best way to see results from a gluten free diet is to try some form of an elimination diet. There is no downside. Complete elimination is paramount, as the body will recognize gluten, even if it is literally a bread crumb. If you do cut down and eliminate gluten from your diet, you may see symptom improvement and subsequently make a big win with a small change. If not, at least you tried something that causes virtually no side effects and the only cost is the time spent learning about gluten. What foods contain gluten? The answer: gluten is hidden in most processed foods and restaurant dishes.

4. Animal Products. If you eat animal products, consider their source. Eat grass-fed beef and wild fish, as these both contain beneficial ratios of healthy, Omega-3 fats. Grain-fed beef and farm-raised fish (farm-raised fish are fed corn among other things, I don't remember corn growing in the ocean!) contain unhealthy, high levels of Omega-6 fats, which cause inflammation and other health problems. Also, watch out for misleading labeling. I have come across frozen fish brands that have the word "wild" in the name, but the tiny print on the back of the package states "farm raised."

5. Healthy Fats. I would recommend getting enough healthy fats in your diet. The French Paradox is a phenomenon seen in the French population that goes against the conventional belief that saturated fat causes heart disease. The French diet has historically been high fat, yet the French population experiences very low

amounts of heart disease. Maybe this is not a paradox at all, given that healthy fats are now being shown to assist with weight loss, as you experience fewer carbohydrate cravings and hunger pains. Additionally, healthy fats are the precursor for important hormones such as estrogen and testosterone, which are vital, especially if you are exercising as part of a weight loss program. Additionally, *many vitamins are fat soluble, meaning they can only be absorbed by eating fat with your meal,* so remember to add a little fat in the form of salad dressing or olive oil to salads and other vegetables. Additionally, I found several studies that link improvements in schizophrenia with high fat diets, also called ketogenic diets.[39,41] Ketogenic diets have been studied for decades, but require physician and lab monitoring. Good sources of healthy fat include avocados, nuts, and wild fish.

6. Fish Oil. The typical western diet leaves individuals deficient in essential fatty acids. Our brains are half fat, so we need to feed our brains the healthy fats they require to function optimally. Omega 3 fatty acids have demonstrated improvements in depression.[42] For the most part, Omega-3 fatty acids are termed essential fatty acids because they cannot be synthesized in our bodies and must be consumed in our food. The easiest way to get these healthy Omega-3 fats into our diets is through a fish oil supplement once or twice a day, taken with meals. This is recommended for anyone suffering with depression, anxiety or other mental health issues. I also recommend placing these supplements in the freezer to keep them fresh. The one major potential side effect of fish oil is thinning of the blood. Before making any dietary changes or adding supplements, discuss with your doctors first.

7. Nutritional Density. Think about the nutritional density of each food before place it in your mouth. This can have a dramatic effect on your physical health and your waistline! First, learn the nutritional content of general food types. Don't make this too difficult. When looking at vegetables, any green veggie is going to

have a bunch more vitamins and minerals than say a white potato or white rice, which are mostly starch. I think the above example illustrates this point well and can be generalized to many scenarios. Another quick and dirty method is to avoid the highly-processed and bleached foods. I will treat myself to a cookie or potato chip from time to time, but a good rule is to cut back on those "empty calories."

8. Super Foods. Another quick and easy way to get nutritionally dense foods is to eat several "super foods" daily. Common ones include avocado, beans, cinnamon, blackberries, blueberries, broccoli, cauliflower, dark chocolate (yes, it's okay in moderation, eating healthy can taste good), leafy greens, walnuts, wild salmon, and green tea (drink this in place of soda). There are a many more, but this will get you started.

9. Probiotics. Consider taking a daily probiotic supplement. Scientific research is now establishing a gut-brain connection. Abnormal gut bacteria influence normal body functioning which contributes to inflammation and obesity. Correcting the healthy balance of bacteria in the intestine helps regulate anxiety, mood, thinking, and pain.[43] The hope in the future will be a specific probiotic prescription based on your genetics and psychiatric symptoms, but we are not there yet.

10. Mindfulness. Those that utilize these strategies enjoy their food more and struggle less to control their eating.[44] Mindful eating practices include:

   a. Eating slower. Eat a normal meal over 20 minutes.
   b. Try eating with non-dominate hand or using chop sticks.
   c. Eat in silence and contemplate your meal's journey, from sun and farm to final preparation. This awareness allows you the time to savor the tastes and textures of your food!
   d. Take small bites and chew well.

e. Before reaching for a snack, ask if you are really hungry. If the answer is no, do something else like going for a walk or go out with a friend.

f. Enjoy the art of gastronomy. Enjoy food with friends, family, and celebration.

11. It's not your fault. It's not your fault if you are struggling with overeating, weight control, or food cravings. Your taste buds have been hijacked. "Food products" have been engineered to make you eat as much as possible and get you hooked! Don't believe me? Perform an online search for the term "food engineering bliss point" and you will be shocked!

12. Buy organic. Why? Non-organic foods are sprayed with a variety of chemicals and pesticides. I learned in medical school that many of these work as neurotoxins, killing living organisms by neuronal damage. There is a correlation between expectant mothers exposed to environmental pesticides and lower IQ and neurodevelopment in their children.[45] Additionally, maternal blood concentrations of pesticides are associated with higher rates of Autism Spectrum Disorders[45] as well as Attention Deficit Disorders (ADHD/ADD), infertility, birth defects, and cancers, as well as other severe medical conditions.[46]

Although we may not be able to eliminate toxic chemicals completely from our diets and environments, we can definitely make some small changes that can drastically limit our exposure. Additionally, studies have shown that organic foods have higher levels of nutrients, probably because industrial and chemically raised foods are grown in soils depleted of nutrients. Luckily, organic foods have significantly dropped in price over the past few years. I personally enjoy an organic green leaf smoothie each morning. Shop and compare, I have found 5 oz. of organic power greens cheaper than the 5 oz. non-organic mixed greens at the big grocery stores. But don't stress out if there is no organic

82

alternative, non-organic fruits and veggies will always be more nutritionally dense and healthier than pizza.

13. Conscientious consumer. At the end of the day, I choose to vote with my wallet. The more we purchase safely and ethically raised foods, the more affordable they become. Become a conscientious consumer. It is impossible to know everything about every product we purchase, but I encourage you to be informed. Make it a regular practice to learn about foods and products. Things such as effects on the environment, ingredient quality, location of origin, and the retailer's practices. You will develop your own criteria when making choices. I choose to shop at locations that give back to local communities and I try to purchase food that is locally raised and free of chemicals. Amazingly, the food industry has already adjusted to consumer demand and has changed some of their practices in just the past few years. Each one of us has the ability to reinforce this change.

14. Check your vitamin levels. Work with your psychiatrist or primary medical physician and discuss laboratory tests to check for vitamin deficiencies. It is important to check for folate and other B vitamins, as well as Vitamin-D. Approximately 80% of my clients have Vitamin-D insufficiency or deficiency. These are simple tests to check. If there are deficiencies, nutritional supplements are easy to add to your daily regimen. Treating such deficiencies will have significant effects on the brain and emotional health.

15. Bonus, Coconut oil. Use organic coconut oil as a natural skin moisturizer. I remember my grandmother would moisturize her hands every day. I was curious which components made it so good for skin. I learned that most moisturizers were made with petroleum products. This didn't make much sense to me, especially when I was old enough to change my car's oil and read that petroleum products can cause cancer. It wasn't until just this past year that I heard about using coconut oil instead. Then the simplicity struck me, you shouldn't put anything on your body

that you wouldn't put in your body. Added benefits of coconut oil include the fact that it is antiviral, antibacterial and antifungal. You can find it as a liquid or solid at room temperature, either is fine. If you use the solid, you will find that it melts quickly on your skin as you gently rub it in. I also find that coconut oil absorbs very quickly without much of an oily residue. So, coconut oil really does appear to be Mother Nature's skin moisturizer.

16. Learn More. If the topic of nutrition interests you, and I hope it does, I encourage you to research more about nutrition on your own!

I think the journalist Michael Pollan summed-up food and nutrition best with these seven words: "Eat food, not too much, mostly plants".

Powerful Effects of Exercise

We have discussed food as a part of holistic treatment; now let's look into another one, exercise. Luckily, exercise has been one thing that we have gotten right, and you can't argue with the results. If it were possible to package exercise into a pill, everyone would want to take it for the benefits. Exercise is good for your body, period. It's also good for your mood. Physical movement has repeatedly shown to decrease depression as well as assist the effectiveness of Selective Serotonin Reuptake Inhibitor (SSRI) antidepressant medications.[48] The antidepressant effects of ongoing exercise continue at a year follow-up.[49] Additionally, we know if you experience more than one episode of depression, you are at risk for another. Again, exercise has you covered, as regular exercise decreases relapse of depression as well.[50] Studies have also repeatedly demonstrated that exercise increases the production of Brain Derived Neurotrophic Factor or BDNF, a protein that supports neurons, increases the number of neuron connections, and encourages growth of new neuronal cells.[51]

We could debate which type of exercise is best. We can all agree, however, that exercise has many beneficial effects such as improving heart and vascular health, sleep, energy, weight loss, blood sugar, depression, and anxiety to name a few. I'm not a stickler for doing an hour-long workout every day. What I recommend is some form of regular body movement. For some it will be going to the gym 3-4 times a week, for others it will be boxing, bicycling, or it may be as simple as getting outside and walking your dog for 10-15 minutes three times a day.

A helpful hint for those that haven't exercised in a while: start slowly. For aerobic exercise, increase the amount of time each day. For strength building, start with light weight and gradually add weight each day. This will help prevent overexertion and injury. Discuss recommendations with your physician based on your personal medical conditions. You may consider working with a personal trainer. Some facilities even have trainers available at no additional cost to the monthly membership.

Did you know that medical research documents that sitting for 8 hours a day cuts your life span! A study that came out in 2012 helped coin the phrase "sitting is the new smoking." Even if you exercise an hour a day, that still doesn't overcome the oppression of being seated and inactive the majority of the day![52] *This is why I say exercise and move!* Get up every hour for 2-3 minutes, go get a glass of water, stretch, and move your body!

When I was attending medical school, I was giving my brain massive workouts every day with the huge amount of information I was learning. After several years I realized that I was working out my mind, but I was neglecting my body. I realized I needed more balance. I require both mind and body activity every day. I notice a pleasant side effect too; my mood, confidence, and even humor improve when I am regularly exercising.

Importance of Sleep

Most people require 7-8 hours of sleep each night. Studies show lack of sleep increases your risk of heart disease and stroke.[53] This also has a direct effect on mental health. We know that sleep is a core symptom of depression, bipolar disorder, and anxiety. Lack of sleep will worsen each condition. Sleep deprivation can actually induce psychotic symptoms in those without mental disorders. Social Rhythms Therapies have also been helpful for depression and bipolar disorders, this therapy includes regular habits that impact the body's daily circadian system through early morning sunlight exposure.[54] Those with a seasonal variant of depression called Seasonal Affective Disorder or SAD, benefit from either bright sun light each morning, or bright light therapy (you can purchase or get a prescription, but the light intensity must be 10,000 lux).[55]

If you are sleeping less than you need, it could be one of the simplest things to correct. I know, your first argument is "I don't have enough time given my work and family duties." But I would argue, that is even more reason for you to make the time, so that when you are working or providing for your family, you are 100% present and more efficient performing each task. Ultimately this will make more time for your reparative rest.

Another important aspect to sleep is how we think about "going to sleep." Some people believe that they need to take a sedating medication that will figuratively put them to sleep "like getting hit over the head with a sledgehammer." Although there are conditions, such as mania, that may require sedating medications, I prefer to think about "going to sleep" as "slipping into sleep". Below are some basic "sleep hygiene" tips to assist with maximum sleep efficiency and "slipping into sleep":

1. Create a bedtime routine and wake up the same time each morning.
2. Keep your bedroom cool, dark, and quiet.
3. Keep your bed for sleep and intimacy only.
4. Avoid alcohol at night.
5. Avoid anything with caffeine after 1pm.
6. Dim the lights in the evening. Computer, tablet, and phone exposure should be minimized in the evening. These bright displays interfere with your body's natural sleep-wake cycle by inhibiting melatonin, a hormone naturally secreted in the brain signaling sleep initiation.

Want more sleep details? Chart your sleep. There are many apps for cell phones. Simply place your phone on your mattress. The alarm will wake you when you are coming out of deep sleep so you won't feel so groggy. It will also give you feedback on the quality of your sleep. There are also all sorts of wearable technology that may also assist with tracking sleep and other health data.

Listen to Your Body

The last physical health topic I wanted to emphasize is how important physical awareness or can be to your overall health. Let's use physical pain as an example. Pain is a very important survival mechanism. It alerts you when you may be in mortal danger, as physical injury could result in death. We are wired to survive. When our flesh is injured, cells are damaged. Damaged cells release inflammatory chemicals which instantly signal our brain: danger!

Now, we may need to react differently to different types of pain, depending on the pain stimulus. Touching a hot stove or a bee sting - both will be telling you the same message - stay away! And you would heal in a matter of days without much problem. What about pain from an incision after surgery? Well, pain is expected, given the tissue damage sustained in surgery, which should heal well. During the initial healing phase, it is perfectly fine to select pain medication. Let's try a third scenario, progressive back pain in someone with Arthritis or Degenerative Joint Disease of the back. Since it is slow and progressive, you don't always know which movements are causing the harm, so it's more difficult to know which movements to avoid. Also, this is a kind of pain you don't always want to mask with opiate pain medication. All that does is numb the pain, all the while possibly re-injuring your back with each movement.

We need to slow down, listen to our body's messaging system and return to a relationship with our bodies. The result is an increase in "body awareness" which can increase your health and functioning. This was found to be the case in a study that used Mindfulness-Based Cognitive

Therapy, where increased body awareness in persons with chronic pain resulted in decreases in pain and depression.[56]

In closing the physical health chapter, I want to leave you with my firm belief in the mind-body connection. Our minds need daily stimulation and our bodies require regular movement. This combination is essential for exceptional health and a sure-fire way to supercharge your wellbeing. *We were born with a mind and body, if you don't use both, they will be slowly taken from you.*

Substance Use and Dependence

Chemical addiction also falls under physical health. More accurately chronic use of substances can rob you of your health. Frequent consumption of any substance places you at increased risk for dependency. Drugs of concern include but are not limited to: nicotine, cannabis, downers such as alcohol and benzodiazepines, stimulants such as caffeine, cocaine and methamphetamines, and opiates.

When does social use of a substance become a disorder? Any one of the following may be a red flag: difficulty cutting down on use, use or intoxication causing risk to physical health, presence of physical tolerance or withdrawal, use of a substance to control emotional distress or social impairment.

There may be a wide-breadth of social impairments. Scholastic or work impairments may surface. This may include absenteeism, declining grades or work performance, or difficulty concentrating. Many times relationships become strained. Financial problems may arise due to the cost of the substance. At the extreme this may lead to stealing, resulting in further strain on family relationships and possibly legal consequences of such actions.

When the physical addiction is severe, individuals may be using the substance just to prevent withdrawal. This is common in alcohol and opiate dependence.

If you or a loved one may be at risk for a substance use disorder, it is imperative to seek medical assistance for withdrawal and to consider substance rehabilitation or rehab.

The good news is that 12 step chemical dependency programs such as Alcoholics Anonymous (AA) and Narcotics Anonymous (NA) employ the psychosocial recovery model. Using the social recovery concepts and the 10 Elements of Recovery in this book are an excellent starting point for a sober life with purpose and meaning. A common complaint from my abstaining clients is, "Now that I'm not spending all of my time chasing and using (enter substance of choice), I don't know what to do with my time." The solution? Incorporate social recovery concepts into your life. Fill your time with healthy social activities that provide you with purpose and meaning. Find ways to rebuild strained relationships. Return to your education or employment goals. Focus on healthy diet and exercise. Chemical dependency is treatable and recovery is possible. I have worked with individuals that have been abstinent for decades!

Questions to assess physical health:

1. Think back to the last time you had a cold or infection. What was your energy level, mood, and ability to concentrate?
2. What is your current physical health status: poor, fair, or good? Are you regularly seeing a primary care doctor and working with them on ways to improve your health? Primary care doctors are trained in preventative medicine, but may not volunteer this information for a number of reasons. If you inquire about these practices, you may be surprised by their response.
3. Do certain foods affect how you feel or your energy level? If so, which foods? You may become more aware of how certain foods make you feel the more you pay attention to your body's subtle cues. Become aware of how different foods affect your energy and mood immediately afterward and a few hours later, specifically sugary foods, carbohydrate heavy meals, and simply overeating.
4. How aware are you of every bite of food you eat? Why are you eating when you do? Are you living to eat or eating to live? Are you eating for emotional comfort? Are you mindlessly filling

your mouth while watching television? Or are you selecting healthy and flavorful options, while savoring each and every bite?

5. How physically active are you? How much are you moving your body each day?

6. How do you feel when you sleep 6-8 hours per night, how do you feel when you get more or less?

7. Are you experiencing any red flags related to substance use: difficulty cutting back, social impairments, health risks, tolerance or withdrawal, using for emotional distress, relationship strain or financial difficulty due to substances?

How to implement better health:

1. Ask your primary care physician which lifestyle changes you can make that will improve your chronic medical illness. Illnesses to consider include, but are not limited to obesity, diabetes, heart disease, lung disease, and autoimmune illnesses.

2. Become more aware of what you eat. Why are you eating? How do certain foods affect your mood and energy? Consider making a food journal or taking photos of each meal and reviewing this with a physician or nutritionist.

3. Make it a routine to engage in at least one physical activity a day, pick a workout buddy, even if it is just a walk in your neighborhood together. Go for a hike or make it a scheduled workout plan at the gym. What will it be?

4. Experiment to find out what type of exercise you like, and try a bunch of things. Many gyms will give you a free trial. Try a beginner's yoga or tai chi class, go for walks or hikes. Find the one or two you like best and make it a part of your regular schedule. What will you try?

5. Make sure you get the proper amount of sleep, start with the above sleep hygiene tips.

6. If substance related issues are present, please speak to a medical or psychiatric professional to discuss treatment options.

Chapter 15:

Element #4 - Purpose

Definition: Purpose - noun - the reason for which something exists or is done, made, used, etc.

Doing...and Living

Recovery is about doing...and living. If you can't take the ideas and concepts in this book and translate them into action, you won't be any better off and nothing will change. When all of the potential elements of recovery were studied, purpose is near the top of the list.[57]

What gets you out of bed every day? What do you look forward to doing every day? You cannot be in recovery without purpose and meaning in your life. I believe our life's purpose is about discovering what excites us. I realize that not everyone has identified their "passion." This process doesn't have to be complex. It could be as simple as getting out of bed the same time each morning, making your meals, visiting with friends, walking your dog, going to a movie, planning a vacation, volunteering, looking for a job or going back to school.

I've repeatedly seen people who have lost their sense of purpose. One cause for this may be mental stress. Take for instance agoraphobia, a severe anxiety disorder that results in such a high level of fear that individuals have difficulty leaving their house. The lack of motivation in some forms of schizophrenia can be so great that the extent of observable activity is nothing more than sitting in front of the TV, drinking coffee, and smoking cigarettes. None of these isolative behaviors are beneficial in the long run. Isolation leads only to stagnation. The only hope for improvement is working on your recovery. Sometimes rest is the best medicine, but after too long, it can turn into a symptom itself and actually become crippling.

One way to combat this is by working with a talk therapist and coming up with new goals each week, to slowly improve your functioning. Or, for the brave soul, you can jump right in, what we call immersion therapy. Regardless of your approach, you will regain your purpose and be on your way to a more fulfilling life.

During my early experience with panic attacks, I coped through escaping anything anxiety provoking. It was common for panic to strike when I was shopping. I could feel the anxiety increasing, the lightheadedness, the shallow breathing, the sweatiness, abdominal distress, feeling on edge, and urge to flee. There were many times when I did just that. While standing in a store checkout line, I would leave my items at the register and make a run for the closest exit. I ended up neglecting social activities due to panic, as it was easier to just avoid interactions. After working on my recovery and using regular breathing exercises, I was able to work through the panic, and after several months, I was able to go anywhere, just as I had before experiencing panic attacks. Because of my recovery, I was able to continue my medical education and my residency training. I wake up each day with purpose. Yes, at times I find it difficult to pull myself from a sound sleep, but I'm able to wake up, knowing I'm helping and educating others to achieve their goals. That is my purpose, in addition to the enjoyment I get from learning and interacting with others.

What's your purpose? How do you spend your day? What do you care the most about in your family and your work? Why do you work? What gives you the most joy? What are your values?

For me, I care the most about listening to each person I see and then providing the best intervention for their situation. I also value self-reliance and the ability to teach these concepts to others. It may be very helpful to spend some time and take a quick inventory of your daily activities. What do you care about most in your life? What are your values? Are you spending time on things that are important? What are your short and long term goals? Are you allocating time each day or week toward your goals? What is going well? What do you need to change?

Education, Work, and Volunteering

Education and work are pivotal factors in recovery. It would be impossible to separate the effects our schools have on the makeup of each and every one of us. Second only to our relationships with our parents and family, school has an influential impact on our social development. It is where we learn appropriate social norms and how to interact with others in society.

Work also shapes us as we move into adulthood. We learn new life skills and, through work, we have a foundation for healthy socialization. It helps sculpt our values and work ethic. Hopefully our work provides personal fulfillment, a sense of accomplishment and joy, as well as providing financial security.

For those lucky individuals, work can become a fulfilling career. Sometimes a career can include both work and education. Erik Erikson, a German-born American psychologist, created a psychological theory composed of 8 stages of healthy psychological development. Each builds on the other and each stage correlates with certain age ranges. In the adulthood stage, roughly between ages 40 and 65, the major psychological crisis revolves around generativity versus stagnation. Those that stagnate are not faced with additional challenges and this usually result in unhappiness. Those who foster generativity and giving back to the next generation tend to flourish.

One profession that has this built-in is teaching. Teaching doesn't need to be limited to the school classroom, but may include any work or interaction where knowledge is transmitted and shared. Not only does education further the instructor's understanding of the information, but it also allows for the individual to tap into something greater than themselves by giving back. This may result from knowing that their knowledge and trade is being passed down to help others for generations to come. For those that are unable to work or are now in retirement, one way to contribute is through volunteerism. Volunteering can be an educational endeavor or something as simple as providing assistance to another person. If this sounds interesting to you, I would recommend starting by researching various volunteer oriented programs in your community. Any of these "giving back" roles are fantastic ways to improve your sense of self-worth and value.

The Pursuit of Happiness

The United States forefathers were on to something which they included in the American Constitution - the pursuit of happiness. Purpose can be as simple as having fun! Sometimes joyful pursuits are all that is required for human fulfillment. As I mentioned in Chapter 8, recovery is about your choices and personal preferences. It's about living a full and rich life. Dine with family. Joke with friends. Attend social affairs. Sing with abandonment. Dance with delight. Read for gratification. Walk in the park. Bask in the sun. Play a favorite sport. Visit a local festival or museum. Experience live theater. Relish poetry. Get lost in music, or better yet, play a song on your favorite musical instrument. Engaging in pleasurable and creative activities increases our happiness. It is what we were made to do.

Questions to explore your daily purpose:

1. Have you been isolated to your bed or apartment due to psychological symptoms?
2. What activities do you enjoy completing each day?
3. What excites you, what is your purpose, what do you want to achieve in your life and what goals and action steps are you following to complete these goals?
4. Think back to a time when you were functioning well or in childhood, what lit you up?

5. What scholastic subject did you naturally excel in or did you like best? How can you pursue further education in that area or put that knowledge to work?
6. Consider writing out a daily or weekly inventory.
7. What is the one thing you would want to accomplish in your lifetime?

Ways to implement Purpose:

1. Find and do at least one thing you enjoy each day. What is it?
2. Can't come up with a purpose or meaning? Ask friends what gives them purpose and meaning, what do they enjoy? You can also discuss this topic with your talk therapist.
3. Make a list of your short term, intermediate, and long-term goals. Break each goal down into individual steps with an appropriate timeline. Then, take action to complete each step.
4. Make a trip to the library. Wander around and thumb through books until you find something that intrigues you, check out a stack of books and start consuming knowledge; it will lead into new worlds of discovery and possibilities.
5. Enroll in a class or seminar about a topic you enjoy.
6. Research jobs you would like to perform.
7. Find a way to "give back" such as sharing knowledge or volunteering.
8. If you still can't figure it out, just pick something fun! Take a painting class, go bowling with a friend, clean your home or get outside for a walk. Goals and activities may change over time, but you need a starting place. What will you try?

Chapter 16:

Element #5 - Community

Definition: Community - noun - a social group of any size whose members reside in a specific locality, share government, and often have a common cultural and historical heritage.

The Evolution of Biology and Communities

We do not live in isolation. We live in an exciting and surprising world. We are social beings. We have been living in various forms of communities since the dawn of human existence. In birth, we require physical and emotional nourishment and care. This led to the formation of the family unit, then tribes, towns, and societies. Communities naturally progressed and developed into cultures which created languages, religions, socialization, governments, commerce, and values. The degree of community integration has been positively correlated to mental wellness.[58] Additionally, mice that were reared in socially rich environments had higher levels of Brain Derived Neurotrophic Factor or BDNF, which is a neuroprotective protein made in neuronal cells.[59] The Release of BDNF leads to the stimulation of new neuronal cells and strengthening those already in existence. So, socially rich environments build stronger brains!

Recreational Sports, Social Groups, and Organizations

As a global society, today we are more connected than ever through mass media and the internet. Although it can be overwhelming at times, we have more options for connecting with preferred "communities" than ever before. For example, say you are newly diagnosed with bipolar disorder. You feel you would benefit from attending a bipolar support group, but the closest in-person meeting is in a city 2 hours away. However, you have the ability to join an online support group. That's just one example of many, but this extends to work, education, social networks, online support groups, and any other hobby or interest you can imagine.

I have lived and worked in various cities in the United States from the eastern coast of Florida to the western coast of southern California. Every time I move to a new city, I research local activities. I attend local groups, both work and recreationally focused. I ask people about their favorite restaurants, parks, and grocery stores. I've joined local recreational sports leagues. I've attended various religious services. I explore each city, both online and in person; I enjoy the adventure! I have used Meetup.com as a way to find local communities of people that enjoy similar interests. Do you like film, culinary arts, or disc golf? There are meetup groups for all of those and more. I've even started my own meetup which has resulted in many new friendships. I had the distinguished honor of leading a wedding ceremony of two good friends that actually met at one of my social events!

Personal Relationships within Your Community

Have you been fostering your social connections or have your relationships been strained? A good sign of mental health is good socialization. It's fascinating that the more social connections outside the brain and the more neuronal connections within the brain, the healthier the mind. Do you have a close friend or confidante? Are you fulfilling your different social obligations as a parent, coach, or team member? Have you been celebrating personal accomplishments, holidays, and celebrations with others? If not, these are great places to start.

We have different levels of identity. We all have a personal and cultural identity. Our cultural identity includes nationality, ethnicity, religion, socioeconomic status and location as well as with the various subcultures we identify. Then there is our personal identity. Personal identity consists of the various roles with which we identify. These roles may include, but are not limited to: parent, sibling, spouse, cousin, grandparent, friend, mentor, employee, team member, and so on. One dimension of recovery is how well you are actively participating in your personal identity roles. Have you been neglecting one or more of these roles?

It may be easiest to begin with family members. You may not have the best relationship with them. Commonly, I have seen family members become estranged as a direct result of stress related to mental illness and related symptoms. But family members know you better than anyone else. Sometimes it takes an outside perspective to help you see around your blind spots. This increases your awareness and can open you up to the bigger picture. Many times it's a therapist, but in recovery, it can also be a friend or family member.

You are the Sum of Your Peers

Peer support specialists, also referred to as recovery coaches, have been an integral part of assisting with the recovery process. Peer specialists are individuals who have lived recovery experiences. They also have been trained and certified to support those struggling with mental illness and guiding them on their own recovery. Since peer specialists have overcome and thrived in spite of their own mental disorders and/or substance use, they can help guide you as well. They provide assistance and feedback based upon their own recovery experiences. If you're interested in becoming a peer specialist or would like to work with a peer specialist, I recommend starting with asking your local mental health providers or searching online.

Additionally, friends and mentors can have dramatic benefits. Jim Rohn, a motivational speaker and business philosopher said, "You are the average of the 5 people you spent the most time with." I believe there is truth in this saying. I have noticed this in my own experience when I have teamed up with a friend to go to the gym; I am more likely to follow-through with a workout. I also notice better results as I feel more supported and pushed to go the extra mile. So if you want to get in shape, pair up with an exercise buddy. If you want to get better grades, study with someone excelling in that subject. If you want to be more religious, go to service with someone that is deep in the faith. You will slowly acquire knowledge and traits of the people with whom you associate. This may change the way you view friendships, not only do you get an ally; you may also gain some of their skill set.

Socializing Feels Good!

Along with my own personal social growth and recovery, I have felt the benefits of socialization more clearly. To me, it is having positive interactions with others that results in laughter, joy, and a sense of wellbeing. Oxytocin is hormone that is released from the brain as a result of social interaction. It is known for encouraging social behavior, social bonding, and is sometimes referred to as the "Love Hormone." This neuropeptide causes that good feeling after positive social interactions.[60] Research has shown that meditation also causes the release of oxytocin.[61] So, if you want to supercharge the benefits of socialization and subsequent oxytocin release, you can spend 30 seconds or several minutes meditating afterwards, replay it in your mind and savor each wonderful moment. The more aware you become and the more often you perform this exercise, the easier it will become.

Although online communities are powerful, they will never replace our local communities. Home is where the heart is. It's also where we buy our local produce and groceries--where we work, play, exercise and socialize. It's made up of our family, friends, co-workers, and peers. How connected are you?

Questions to help identify your communities:

1. Can you make a list of each activity you participate in a week?
2. Where do you go?
3. With whom do you meet and interact?

4. What are your interests and hobbies?
5. What is your cultural identity? Personal identity?
6. What roles have you neglected? Which ones have you fostered?
7. Which groups and organizations are you a part of, both in person and online?

Ways to increase your community connections:

1. Many cities have local Psychosocial Clubhouses. These are places to go, have meaningful relationships, and engage in meaningful work. Research some in your area. Which will you visit?
2. Pick a personal identity role and get social. What role are you going to select? Call a friend and plan an activity--go for a walk, hike, go to a family member's sports game, attend that social event you've been invited to, or support a local charity or cause. Who are you going to call?
3. Schedule a group celebration, for yourself or a friend, after a completed goal. How will you celebrate?
4. Search for local events in your community. Newspapers usually feature upcoming activities or search online. Many will even be free. What did you find?
5. Find your best friend or confidant; it could save your life! Who will it be?
6. Practice savoring positive social encounters. Try it now, pick a previous joyful experience and reminisce on those good thoughts and feelings for 1 minute. How do you feel afterwards?

Chapter 17:

Element #6 - Non-Linear

Definition: Non-Linear - noun – not a straight line or path

Life is full of change; change is growth. Embrace change and growth and you will embrace recovery. How boring would life be if there was not change? Life is based on cycles of duality. Day and night, waxing and waning tides, sun shining through the rain and clouds, the cycle of life from birth to death. No person in the history of the world has thus far escaped the human experiences of life--loss of relationships, death of loved ones, or scholastic and work challenges. The power of this element of recovery is knowing that a step back can actually be a step forward. By realizing the ability to anticipate small slides during periods of life stressors and "growing pains", you can hasten your ability to work through each obstacle.

Success is Learning from Experience

Although trial and error are inevitable in life, western society views mistakes and "failure" as a bad thing. Failure can be one of life's greatest teachers, it provides us with valuable feedback. We must learn from these experiences. Failure is not the error; the error is not learning from the failure. No successful person is free of failure. The accomplished person learns from their experiences. Life itself is a journey, one that demands we work daily, along life's bumpy road, to be successful. There is also a concept of "grit" or "iron will". There is a correlation between the ability to stick with something and success. People that have a purpose will keep getting up, no matter how many times they are knocked down. For it will be the person that gets up that will accomplish their goal.

The ups and downs of life can feel like a roller coaster ride. But aren't those hills and valleys what makes a roller coaster fun? Millions of people travel to amusement parks and wait in line for hours for roller coaster rides all over the world to experience this thrill. Do you think it's possible to change your point of view from one that is scared of the ride to excitement?

I was working towards my goal of becoming a physician when anxiety struck. When it first hit, I felt overwhelmed and experienced impending doom. It was suffocating. But slowly, over the following weeks and months, the intensity lessened. Slowly, there was more time between attacks and the episodes themselves were becoming shorter in duration. I was on an upward swing. Then came the setbacks, new problems popped up like panic attacks in public, especially while shopping. As a result, I adjusted my schedule and routine around the anxiety. There is only one guarantee with recovery; it has its ups and downs. The hope is that by learning about your illness, by working in your recovery, that you will have more ups than downs. Although you know that there will be rough patches, you will go on to see another fantastic day and live life to your fullest given the curveballs that life throws at you.

Recovery Graphs

I think a helpful way to think about the non-linear aspect of recovery is to visualize it as a chart. At times it can feel like it is one step forward two steps back. My hope is that one, three, and six months down the line, things will be better than they are now. It is your life, future, and recovery. The only barrier is your inaction.

The first graph on the next page, entitled Standard Treatment Improvement, is what I have frequently observed in working with people that are receiving standard psychiatric treatment or no treatment at all. As you can see, there are ups and downs, but the total change is zero.

106

Strandard Treatment Improvement

An ideal recovery, if plotted on a chart, would be a straight line. As illustrated below. One would be excelling in an upward direction, always growing and improving. But a straight line tends to be quite dull, devoid of learning opportunities and meaningful life experiences.

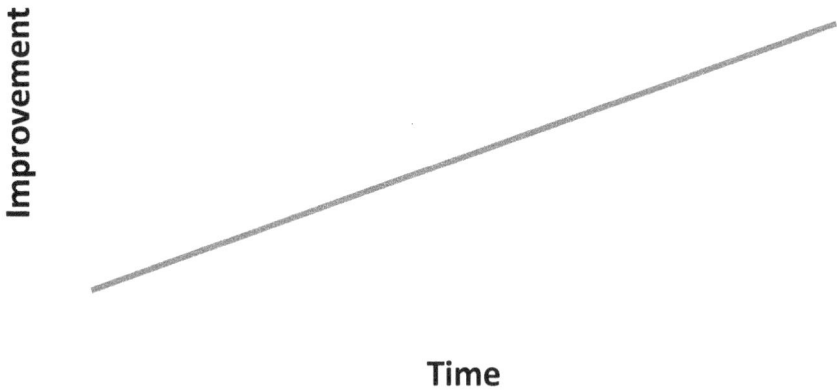

Ideal Recovery (Not Real World)

A chart like the one below, entitled Realistic Recovery Path to Improvement is a bit more practical. It is a stair-step approach with incremental improvements. Yet, there may be times where you feel you are going backwards. Don't worry, that is the time of learning and usually when the next breakthrough is around the corner. It is a more accurate representation of what a person truly experiences in recovery. It is also much more exciting.

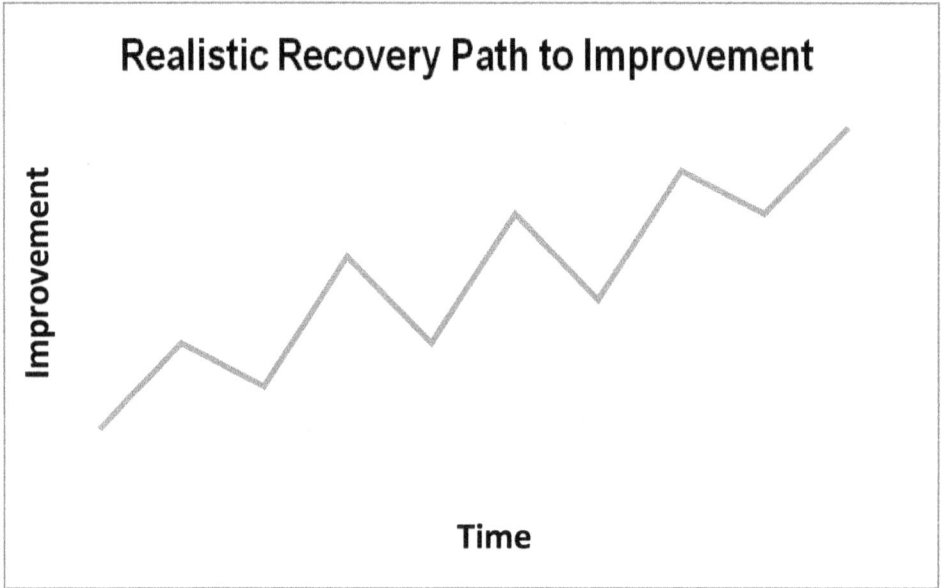

Realistic Recovery Path to Improvement

Improvement (vertical axis) — *Time* (horizontal axis)

I think we all can identify with setbacks. Remember that the setbacks are actually important. Be willing to *allow yourself this precious space* for rest, processing, and the growth that is soon to come. For just as we need sleep for our minds and bodies to repair, we also need to allow for rest in our life for the next growth spurt.

One way to access an additional layer within this concept is to actually track your symptoms. One way to do this is simply writing down your symptoms in a journal. There are also many free anxiety and mood trackers available. Some programs monitor symptoms such as sleep, irritability, mood, and appetite. Some even allow for customization options like recording social interactions or other notes. This allows you and your mental health practitioners to review your progress in a very interesting way while providing a mechanism for you to identify obstacles getting in the way.

There are no mistakes, only opportunities for learning what hinders and what improves your recovery. There is always hope for a better tomorrow.

This reminds me of a country song by Rodney Atkins titled "If You're Going through Hell" (keep on going, don't slow down, if you're scared don't show it, you might get out before the devil even knows you're there). There is actually a whole lot going on in those lyrics. I'm sure persons in recovery would testify to this advice. Keep on going, there is a light at the end of the tunnel!

Nonlinear recovery questions and comments:

1. Can you look back on your psychological journey with mental illness and see different periods of declining and improved functioning?
2. How has your diagnosis served you? What have you learned from your illness?
3. Remember that just as in life, recovery has ups and downs. Don't let a bump in the road throw you off your recovery. Pick yourself up, dust yourself off, and keep going!

Chapter 18:

Element #7 - Hope: There Is Hope of Recovery

Definition: Hope - noun - the feeling that what is wanted can be had or that events will turn out for the best.

"Hope is a good thing, maybe the best of things" – Andy Dufresne

From *The Shawshank Redemption*

Many times when we are experiencing increasing stress we can feel completely strained. We may have the belief that there is no way out of this feeling or situation, which can lead to thoughts of hopelessness. When the brain gets stressed, we may experience a form of tunnel vision that prevents us from asking for help and keeps us from seeing the countless opportunities for improvement. Although there is no cure for any mental illness, there are extensive amounts and forms of mental health treatments, including social recovery. These treatments help alleviate symptoms, restore functioning, health, and well-being. The important thing to know is that there is hope for recovery in spite of mental illness. Hope works by enabling individuals to take action and by preventing discouragement during times of setbacks.

As I am writing this, I just finished meeting with a client. I initially met Mark in the Intensive Care Unit because he had taken an overdose of pills in a suicide attempt. Luckily, he survived, but only after having been intubated and on a ventilation respirator to keep him breathing and alive. He told me that he was tired of dealing with schizophrenia, bipolar disorder, and psychiatric medications for the past 30 years. He reported a worsening depressive episode for the past 6 months. He had been contemplating suicide for that long as well, until he ultimately took the overdose. He was agreeable to a voluntary psychiatric hospitalization after I explained how I believed I could help.

On the first day in the psychiatric unit, I met with him and his family. I informed them about recovery and gave them handouts on the topic. We discussed his previous medications and his experience with each. Together, we devised an individualized medication regimen. Upon discharge, Mark thanked me for my assistance with his treatment. He told me that when he first met me, he couldn't imagine feeling so well. His mood was improved and stable and he had purposeful goals to focus on for the next 3-6 months. Above all else, he told me he was more hopeful now than he had been in the past 4-5 years! I believe this was a direct result of our recovery discussions more than anything else. Yes, the medications are important, but he has been on some form of medication for the past 30 years. It was the hope of recovery that gave him a renewed purpose for living. *Recovery provides hope!*

I know that there is hope. I have witnessed it in others lives, as well as my own. Mark is not the only person that has started his healing journey, but he is an excellent example. I have personally worked with countless people when they have been in the depths of desperation, but I have also accompanied them on their road to recovery and have repeatedly seen people improve their lives and functioning. With the new social treatment of recovery, in combination with other traditional medications and psychotherapy, there is more hope than ever.

Evidence for Recovery:

Recovery Rates for Schizophrenia

Schizophrenia is a psychotic illness by definition. Persons with schizophrenia may experience symptoms such as false beliefs, disorganized thinking, perceptual disturbances, such as seeing objects or hearing sounds that are not present in the environment, social withdrawal, and lack of facial expression. Please keep in mind that not every symptom is required for the diagnosis of schizophrenia and each person's severity and symptoms vary.

Historically, schizophrenia has been regarded as one of the most severe psychiatric diagnoses. Schizophrenia has long been believed to cause a progressive, deteriorating process. This is just not the case. There have been 30 studies over a 30-year span between 1969 to 1999 conducted in 30 countries that have consistently demonstrated recovery rates of individuals with psychotic disorders are between 45 and 65%![62] These rates are based on symptoms and ability to live and function independently. What's more, those studied did not receive recovery education and many received no treatment at all!

Larry Davidson is a PhD psychologist and director of the Yale Program for Recovery and Community Health. He has published numerous studies on recovery over the past two decades. He is one of the chief proponents and educators of recovery. This is his summation of recovery in schizophrenia:

> We then examine the ten long-term follow-up studies of serious mental illnesses that lay the groundwork for the possibility of recovery, and demonstrate consistently that 50 to 60% of each sample were able to experience significant improvements in the illnesses and in their lives. These studies contain many important findings, including a broad heterogeneity in outcome; early course fluctuations followed by later decreases in severity; the failure of traditional indicators to predict course or outcome over the longer term; the existence of multiple pathways to recovery, including the restoration of social and occupational functioning; and the fact that many people do not continue to take psychiatric medications for the entirety of their lives as we have come to expect.[63]

There are two points I want to highlight from Dr. Davidson's quote above. One is that individuals with psychotic illnesses may experience significant and meaningful recovery. Two is that individuals that are prescribed any type of medication, psychiatric or medical, have high rates of medication non-adherence. Not taking medications as prescribed is a big problem because the individual is not maximizing their biological intervention, which in turn short changes the very condition they are hoping to treat. Fortunately in psychotic illnesses there are medications that don't need to be taken every day. These long acting injectable medications only require dispensing every few weeks or months. I believe these medications can help individuals achieve recovery more quickly, allowing them to focus on their social recovery. This goes back to my idea of stacking the bio-psycho-social therapies on top of each other, enabling you to get the most out of your treatments. Although these medications are not for everyone, it's worth discussing long acting injectable options with your psychiatrist or mental health provider.

Don't think you know anyone in recovery from hearing voices? Think again, Sir Anthony Hopkins won the Academy Award in 1991 for his portrayal of Hannibal Lecter in movie *The Silence of the Lambs*. He declared a history of hearing voices during an interview in 1993. He seems to be doing just fine in his acting career despite the challenging distraction of auditory hallucinations.

I think the biggest take-away from this is that even in some of the most historically challenging diagnoses and symptomology, significant recovery has occurred and is happening. Diagnoses that were once thought of as a prison sentence, now need to be re-considered and seen in a whole different light, given the increasing amount of global data showing these astounding recovery rates. Remember, this is in the setting of no psychosocial recovery education. Imagine the potential of someone diagnosed with schizophrenia implementing the elements of recovery into their life. The rates of recovery in schizophrenia could be even higher!

Persons in Recovery

I have come across many different individuals that have found recovery. Patricia Deegan is a PhD psychologist as well as a person in recovery with schizophrenia. She is also a vocal advocate for recovery. During my fellowship I read *The Center Cannot Hold: My Journey Through Madness*, a memoir by Elyn Saks. She chronicles her beginning and ongoing struggle with schizophrenia. Elyn is an exceptional example of a person in recovery, as she shares her challenges going through law school, then completing her psychoanalytic degree. She continued to work and write despite her psychiatric condition. Another powerful book was written by Kay Jamison, *An Unquiet Mind: A Memoir of Moods and Madness*. She tells of her erratic experiences with bipolar disorder. She reveals how she navigated a demanding work schedule and personal relationships in the throes of mania and severe depression. All of the following persons discovered recovery on their own through trial and error. But you know what, they found it. So can you, but you have a secret weapon. You have a map in your hands. Others have found their recovery, now go and find yours.

Recovery from Suicidal Thoughts

Self-preservation and survival are some of the most primal human drives. When suicidal thoughts and impulses occur, it is most commonly an indication of severe depression, regardless of the specific diagnosis. There are approximately 33,000 completed suicides in the U.S. annually, which is twice the number of homicides. That translates into more than 1 person every 15 minutes.[64] Suicide is a difficult topic for most people to discuss, but something mental health professionals encounter on a daily basis. As a medical physician and psychiatrist, my first duty is to do no harm, which includes preventing the loss of life. Unfortunately, I have witnessed the devastation that a completed suicide leaves in its wake. Suicidal thinking is a serious symptom which requires an evaluation by a psychiatrist or other mental health professional for immediate safety and treatment. If you find yourself or someone you know struggling with these dangerous thoughts, you can also call the National Suicide Prevention Lifeline, 24/7, toll free: 1-800-273-TALK (8255).

Common treatments for suicidal thoughts and their associated disorders include medication and counseling interventions. Cognitive Behavior Therapy (CBT), a psychotherapy that looks at how thoughts, feelings and behaviors are related, and Interpersonal Psychotherapy, a therapy that focuses on how relationships affect moods, have proven effective in treating various mood and personality disorders. Additionally, CBT can reduce risk factors such as hopelessness and suicidal thoughts. Dialectical Behavioral Therapy is a specialized psychological intervention that reduces suicidal thinking and self-injurious behaviors in those diagnosed with Borderline Personality Disorder. The development of a crisis safety plan may also be beneficial. Safety plans are usually created together with your mental health provider and provide a guide to follow when unsafe thoughts occur. Alcohol and other illicit substance use are known risk factors for suicide. Therefore, treating co-occurring addiction is a must.

A study of over 2,800 participants highlighted the importance of socialization in decreasing mental illness in those who have seriously contemplated suicide. It found those individuals who had a "confidant" (which I would define as a supportive person that you trust and feel comfortable sharing your thoughts and feelings) were *seven times more likely to have complete mental health recovery!*[65]

This is a big deal. Medication and psychotherapy are both very important components of your treatment. Imagine, though, the significance of boosting your response seven-fold by simply adding a supportive person that you can trust and communicate with; thereby reducing your likelihood of self-harm and supercharging your recovery process.

There is only one question to ask yourself, *who's going to be your confidant?* Hope is one of the core components of mental health recovery. Yet, hope is absent when suicidal thinking is present. I can't think of anything more positive, or that provides more hope, than knowing recovery is possible, even with the most severe mental health symptoms.

If there is hope for recovery from one of the most severe and lethal symptoms in mental illness, then there is hope for recovery from all mental illness.

Faith and hope are powerful tools. They have gotten mankind through insurmountable challenges throughout history. Hope is the light at the end of the tunnel. You may have experienced various setbacks through your dealings with mental stress thus far. This can cause people to experience intense hopelessness. But, if you get nothing else from this book, I want to impress upon you that recovery is possible and people do recover.

Still struggling with this element of recovery? Pick up a copy of the book, *Man's Search for Meaning* by Viktor Frankl; it documents Frankl's survival in a Nazi concentration camp. I can't imagine a more hopeless situation, yet Frankl was able to find hope while he was engulfed by death and dying. He went on to live a full life, in spite of his inhumane experience as a Holocaust survivor.

Questions about hope:

1. What things have caused you to feel hopeless in the past?
2. When was there a time in your life that you were hopeful?
3. What things have given you hope in the past?
4. What does hope feel like?

Chapter 19:

Element #8 - Personal Responsibility

Definition: Responsibility - noun - the state or fact of being responsible, answerable, or accountable for something within one's power, control, or management.

Take Charge of your Recovery!

The Key Factor to your recovery is...you! Your recovery is your own. Who is responsible for your recovery? You! You must be willing to take charge of your recovery. Regardless of the best psychiatrist, the most compassionate therapist, an excellent treatment team, and a loving and supportive social network, no one can put you on your road to recovery other than yourself. Only you can choose to recover. Interestingly, a study found that individuals prescribed psychiatric medications for years with continued severe anxiety or depression symptoms actually experienced better results with lower medical costs when they added social recovery to their treatment.[66]

Recovery is an Active Process

Recovery requires effort, it's an active process. Take responsibility and make the needed changes to your life, otherwise things will continue to be the same. Lack of motivation and passivity are the potential obstacles to your success. Inactivity puts you at the mercy of other's wishes, plans, and desires. Regain your sense of control and become a driving force for your goals, future, and life.

The Five Stages of Change

Your ability to initiate anything new in your life depends on where you are in the spectrum of change. There are 5 psychological stages of change. You may have encountered this model if you have ever tried to change a habit, for example to quit smoking. The 5 stages are Pre-contemplation, Contemplation, Preparation, Action, and Maintenance. We have all gone through the stages of change in our lifetime. Many times at the pre-contemplation stage, we become paralyzed with fear. You may have been ignoring the issue so long, that hearing of it is so overwhelming, the only way to cope is through denial. Denial is a basic psychological defense mechanism; when we tell ourselves the problem doesn't exist. And that may be okay sometimes. We all work through these stages at our own pace. Our subconscious mind slowly works on the problem. Sometimes we need a break. Time is healing. Return to the issue after the dust has settled. This step back allows us to approach the topic with clearer thinking and may result in the ability to take the next step.

Change is a Choice

Only you can decide to change. If you do not change, things are likely to stagnate. No one else is going to fight for your recovery other than you; others can support you, but at the end of the day it begins and ends with you. I don't usually make future predictions, but if you choose to continue on your current path without purposeful change, I would bet that nothing will change for you.

As my mother told me growing up, you can take a horse to the fountain, but you can't make him drink. This is true with recovery. I've seen countless people carried and dragged into treatment by loved ones when the individual is not yet ready to engage in mental health treatment. Many times loved ones are doing what they believe is the right thing. This may result in an emergency psychiatric evaluation and potentially lifesaving interventions. There is no better time to decide to change than the present moment. Are you ready to take the first drink of water?

You're in the Driver's Seat

Are you ready for change? Are you willing to prepare, plan and then follow through with your recovery plan? The odds are good, given that you are reading this book and have invested time to learn about recovery. Now that you possess the knowledge of recovery, you are now accountable to yourself. You are now ready to begin your journey of recovery. What is truly unique about the recovery model is that you are in the driver's seat; you are in control. You set the course and steer. You may make a wrong turn from time to time, but part of the recovery process is ongoing course correction. Trial and error. You didn't find your favorite meal until after trying many dishes, right? Sometimes the wrong turn allows you to make new discoveries.

Being the director of your recovery is imperative; it empowers you. You not only have a say in its development, you also have the final word. The buck literally stops with you. But, to borrow a line from my favorite superhero Spiderman, "with great power comes great responsibility."

Become Your Own Advocate

This means you must become your own advocate. You must speak up for yourself and your treatment. You achieve this by requesting and sharing your preferences, hopes, and goals. All of which should be driving forces for your recovery. Share this with your providers, as well as friends and family members. As a result, you may find they will support you and may even make suggestions that you haven't considered. *You have a personal responsibility to someone in your recovery, and that responsibility is to yourself.*

Taking responsibility for your recovery is an important task. It may feel daunting, but don't fret. Take some time to process and come back to it when you're ready.

How to begin implementing personal responsibility in your recovery:

1. Have you been answering the questions at the end of each chapter? The answers are your recovery plan. You have already begun taking responsibility by selecting the things you want and, just as important, what you don't want, in your recovery by answering and implementing your recovery preferences.

2. An additional approach is to take some time to sit down and write out your goals. Describe how you would like your ideal day or life to look like. This will give you a foundation to begin. Then make smaller goals, list what resources you require and what you need to add or remove from your life to achieve that improved level of functioning.

3. You may ask a trusted friend or mentor for guidance. A certified peer specialist could be a powerful advisor, as they support persons in recovery, while being in recovery.

4. Remember, you are in charge of your recovery. Are you putting enough time into this important job? Select a time each month to review your recovery goals, progress, and then make subsequent additions and new goals.

Chapter 20:

Element #9 - Self-Determination

Definition: Self-Determination - noun – determination by oneself or itself, without outside influence.

Your Recovery; Your Way

There is no "one way" to recover. Your recovery will be completely unique and different than anyone else's. Certain elements of recovery will resonate with you, others won't. Each element of recovery has so many variables, which will combine and become your unique individual recovery signature. There are also numerous ways to implement recovery. You may choose to focus on one element at a time and make small changes. Conversely, you may wish to dive straight in and make many changes at once. This is all up to you. You know yourself best and how you adjust to change. You may choose to build on current strengths in each domain, or you may decide to start in areas of perceived weakness or deficiency, working to strengthen those foundations.

How can you begin to individualize your recovery? Let me present you with a biological intervention example. Being a psychiatrist, I select medication therapies based on each person's individual symptoms. I start by evaluating many areas including medical co-morbidities. I review all current medications and supplements, reviewing for potential side effects. I consider family members that have either responded, or not responded, to certain medications. My point in all this is to show the individualized approach I take in selecting each medication and dose for each person. Sometimes I have found the first medication trial is effective and free of side effects. Other times it may require trial and error in finding the right combination based on your specific biology. Make it a priority to discuss your medications with your psychiatrist.

We can apply that same principal to psychotherapy. There are various forms of talk therapy. Interestingly, the greatest determination of talk therapy's success is how the individual feels towards the therapist. Broadly speaking, when an individual finds a "good fit" with a therapist, better outcomes typically ensue.

Diversity within the Elements of Recovery

The amount of social therapy treatment options are limited only by your creativity. You start with the 10 core elements. You then choose the various activities based on your preferences. The best part is that you get to pick what you want in your recovery and what you want to leave. You get to envision what you want in your life, and then go to work to make it happen. Because of the infinite number and various combinations, every person's recovery will be unique.

You will personalize and individualize your recovery. Your mental health prescriber can assist you in finding an appropriate medication trial. You may consider finding a talk therapist. If so, you may wish to ask your prescriber for a psychotherapy referral, or your friends and family members may have a recommendation. You may find a 12-step support group, given your individual factors, which may include Alcoholics Anonymous or Narcotics Anonymous. You may seek a Sponsor or Peer Specialist. You may want to add groups to help in certain areas such as social skills. Additionally, the National Alliance on Mental Illness (NAMI) is a great support for family members of recovering individuals. NAMI provides online resources and there are chapters in every state.

You may have loved ones supporting you throughout your recovery. These individuals can support you through the tough times or simply help with transportation to appointments or classes. You may choose to include work, volunteering, or education goals into your recovery.

This is the fun part of recovery: you get to rediscover your curiosity. You get to try things without a thought of fear or failure. Each experience is a new opportunity to find joy and happiness. You get to release your inner adventurer. So, what's going to be the next thing you try?

Making your Recovery Individualized:

1. Work with your mental health prescriber to find the right medication combination that's right for you.
2. Consider talk therapy and ask around for recommended therapists to find a good fit.
3. Make a list of the people you want to involve who will be supportive in your recovery.
4. Consider a support group. Start by searching local or online support groups.
5. Find an area in your life that you want to learn more about and make a commitment and follow through. It might be enrolling in that class you have been thinking about for years, signing up for a fun social group or volunteering for a good cause. What will it be?
6. By selecting various individual facets within each recovery element, you will be effectively individualizing your recovery. It's built-in!

Chapter 21:

Element #10 - Spirituality: Spiritual and Religious Practice in Recovery

Definition: Spirituality - noun - the quality or fact of being spiritual.

One way to supercharge your recovery is to include spiritual or religious practices. Divine practices go hand-in-hand with healing. These practices allow you to reconnect and tap into the infinite universal life source. Benefits include increasing your compassion for others, awareness of self, seeing things from different perspectives, learning from others, guiding your ethical compass, adding to your sense of community, as well as quieting the mind. This allows individuals to find healthy ways of communicating and interacting with others. In fact, persons that identify themselves as highly religious or spiritual have fewer depressive symptoms.[67] Additionally, spirituality is also a significant predictor of recovery from depression after 1-year.[68]

Religion and Social Functioning

I experienced an example of religion's utility in uncovering a psychological condition first hand in one of my learning opportunities overseas. In my last year of psychiatry residency training, I was fortunate enough to participate in an international psychiatric rotation in the Sultanate of Oman, a country on the Arabian Peninsula. The psychiatrists I worked with gave me some social and cultural tips that would help me uncover psychological dysfunction. Being a predominately Muslim country, individuals who deviate from their regular practice of five daily prayers could be an indication of worsening mental health symptoms. Attending religious services decreased subsequent depression, while depression itself leads to subsequent lower levels of religious service attendance.[69]

Beliefs and Practices

Religion and spirituality can be further divided into beliefs and practices. Beliefs are powerful and can absolutely affect your emotions and functioning. What type of world do you believe that you live in? What personal views changed over the course of your lifetime? What spiritual or religious practices would you like to learn more about?

Some people find themselves in the depths of despair and anxiety, often as a result of, or co-occurring with spiritual distancing. Interestingly, spirituality and religiousness have been associated with a lower risk of suicide.[70] If you find that your religious practices have lapsed, it may be as simple as to returning to your regular spiritual activities. For example, someone raised Muslim, Jewish, Hindu, Buddhist, or Christian may choose to attend religious services. You could incorporate daily prayer back into your life. You may find new practices, such as meditation or reconnecting with nature.

One commonality among most religions is the belief in a higher power. This is a reminder that anything is possible and offers hope. Additionally I believe the key to spiritual and religious growth is the process itself. You are not just a Hindu, Christian, Jew, or Muslim, you are one that practices such beliefs. There is no end to spiritual achievement; there is only ongoing spiritual growth and practice. This is one realm in which the old saying is true, if you don't regularly use it, you lose its benefit. Spiritual and religious daily practice can be very powerful and transformative. It can truly spur one's recovery. Of course, these practices may be done individually or in group congregations. Many times it can be even more powerful in groups. So, call your friends and family and go to a religious service or on a hike together.

Heightened Consciousness

Many spiritual and religious beliefs have to do with the fact that we are all connected on various levels. Religious and spiritual growth is a process which results in this higher consciousness: that we come from the same source or place, that we all live on this earth together, and that we are all brothers and sisters of humanity. When you are aware and understand this connection, you can no longer ignore the fact that you are accountable to each and every living being and even the earth itself. You begin to realize that each and every action you perform directly impacts others, which ultimately impacts yourself.

Ways to implement religious practice and spirituality:

1. Do you already have a strong religious background? You may select re-integrating your previous practices. It may be more enjoyable to practice with loved ones.
2. No previous religious background? No problem. Did you ever wonder about certain religious or spiritual practices? Ask someone about their religious practices or pick up a book on the topic to find out more. Ask to join your friend the next time they go to a service.
3. Many religions and cultures use physical reminders for prayer. These may include rosary, prayer or worry beads. Consider using an external reminder for your daily prayer practices.

Gratitude

If you don't have a strong religious or spiritual orientation, gratitude may be for you. The easiest way I know how to tap into your spiritual self is through gratitude. Gratitude is a simple, yet powerful tool. People that regularly practice active gratitude tend to be happier and more joyful. Gratitude has been found to have direct effects on an individual's self-esteem, depression and even suicidal thoughts.[71] You can practice gratitude in various ways. Some examples include daily prayer, a daily or weekly written journal, or expressing your gratitude to yourself or others each day. The trick is to avoid rote reciting of words in an emotionless state. Instead, try expressing gratitude by feeling that gratitude, and staying with that feeling, while in the moment. Gratitude is an active process!

Easy Daily Gratitude Practice Suggestions:

1. Keep a gratitude journal. Write 3 things that you are grateful for each morning when waking or before bed.
2. Find a gratitude object. Maybe a gratitude rock or crystal. Passionately recite three things you are grateful for each time you put it in and out of your pocket.
3. Consider including gratitude as part of your daily prayers or before meals.

Chapter 22:

Putting It All Together

Do you know what successful people do? They create a plan and they stick to it! Arnold Schwarzenegger didn't become Mr. Olympia by just going to the gym and working out. He had a plan which included how much weight and the number of repetitions he would perform for each exercise. He followed a strict diet, and he made sure to get enough rest each night.

What about financial investments? Any financial advisor would ask you questions about your investment goals, whether you're discussing your 401K, IRA, or stock and bonds. They would want to know your investment timeframe, the amount of risk you're comfortable taking, the amount available to invest, your experience with investing and other questions. The investment advisor will then tailor an individual investment plan to help you achieve your goals.

If you still don't believe me about how important plans are, ask any doctor. You may have wondered about the thought process a doctor goes through when preparing your specific treatment. Every time you see a doctor, he or she uses a specific formula. They ask you about the reason for the visit and any other pertinent history, they then perform a physical exam, after which they come up with the most likely diagnosis. And then…you guessed it, their plan for your treatment! Yes, every single patient I see, have seen, and will see in the future, has a plan. I document a plan in each client's medical chart which I use to help guide their care.

Whether it is bodybuilding, investing, medicine or any other endeavor, I think you would agree having a plan is crucial. Having a plan is going to get you to your goal the fastest with the best results.

Another great thing about plans is that they takeout the guesswork. You don't have to continuously question what you are doing. Before you start, do your research, come up with your strategy and then all that is left is to execute your plan.

One problem people struggle with is making the plan. Here is the good news, you can make it fun. This is your recovery plan; you can fill your recovery with whatever you want. And the best part of recovery is that it is social, so the more fun activities you fit into your recovery plan, the better your recovery will go.

Recovering from mental illness is not easy, but you don't have to continue to struggle. You now know what you can do to take out the guesswork and put you on a path to success. Below is my four-step system to create and follow up on your recovery journey.

Creating Your Recovery Plan

1. Inventory. Make an inventory of where you are with each element of recovery. Write down at least one or two things you want to do for each of the 10 elements of recovery. If you have been answering the questions at the end of each chapter, you have already completed this step!

2. Goals. Set goals for each item. *The key here is to be specific with dates and times.* Maybe it's drinking a green smoothie *every morning for breakfast* or exercising *three times a week immediately after work.*

3. Implement. Execute and follow through on your above recovery goals. I personally like posting notes to help me remember. Consider placing your recovery goals somewhere you will see them each day, such as your bathroom mirror or on the fridge.

4. Repeat. Every few weeks or months you will want to reassess your recovery plan and goals. Take another inventory, set new goals for yourself and then implement. Recovery is an ongoing

process. This is also the time to reflect on what you have accomplished and celebrate your achievements!

Recovery Revolution Worksheet

I have created a Recovery Revolution Worksheet, which collects all the questions from each chapter listed in a word document. I have made it accessible for free to anyone on my website. Simply go to PaulRashidMD.com or scan the below QR Code to download and print.

Chapter 23:

Closing Thoughts and Clinical Pearls

We're All in Recovery

Aren't we all in recovery? If you're breathing, you're in recovery; it's part of "Life's Journey." We experience difficult challenges during our lifetimes. Excessive levels of stress have the potential to cause debilitating symptoms. You may not have been aware in the past, but you now know that you hold the keys to unlock the chains of mental illness. It all goes back to awareness, education, and regular self-care and self-nurturing. You must clear out the mental weeds, while also cultivating healing mental seeds.

Roles and Goals

Christine Rufener PhD, one of my Psychosocial Rehabilitation Advisor's favorite slogan for Recovery is two words: Roles and Goals. Eric Granholm PhD says to *make your roles your goals*. Basically, by fulfilling your different roles (parent, friend, employee, etc.), while continually cultivating and working toward your goals, recovery will naturally follow.

Mental Illness Silver Linings: My Adaptive Theory of PTSD

Strive to see the silver lining in your situation. Many times life presents us with challenges when growth is needed. Ignoring the underlying issues may just perpetuate the symptoms.

In retrospect, anxiety served me in my life. Initially, I reacted by pulling back, isolating, and becoming more rigid with my schedule, but only temporarily. Ultimately I learned to be less rigid and become more flexible. I also believe that anxiety is a protective factor. It keeps me accountable, aids me in completing my work within acceptable time frames, and with high quality.

You may be saying to yourself, "Dr. Paul that may be the case for you, but not for the trauma I have endured." I would like to address a potentially very challenging diagnosis, Post-Traumatic Stress Disorder, or PTSD. (Author's note, I have heard a new possible name for PTSD, Post-Traumatic Stress Syndrome or PTSS. As the Diagnostic and Statistical Manual of Mental Disorder or DSM 5 still uses the PTSD name, I will continue to refer to it as this, but PTSS may be a less stigmatizing term for future use.) PTSD is a condition that is a result of a life-threatening event. Such events may include a motor vehicle accident, natural disaster, physical or sexual assault, or combat. Of note only approximately 15% of persons exposed to a trauma go on to develop a diagnosis of PTSD.[72] Symptoms may include re-experiencing the event, avoidance behaviors, adverse effects on mood and alterations in arousal and reactivity. Hypervigilance is an enhanced state of threat detection. Persons exposed to combat may experience PTSD with symptoms of hyperarousal. I have worked with individuals with both combat and non-combat related PTSD.

It is common for my clients with PTSD to tell me that they visually scan public areas, such as in crowds or prefer to sit with their backs against the wall in restaurants. Family members or friends may think, "What unusual behavior!" when they don't understand the underlying protective purpose of this behavior. There is a rationale: the affected person is stuck in survival mode, surveying their environment and assessing the threat level. This can be debilitating for those suffering with PTSD.

If you look closely, there is a silver lining. Healing comes from finding meaning. What is the meaning of PTSD? I believe the purpose of PTSD is very significant, and not just to those dealing with PTSD, but all of humanity. You see, the only way we survived as a species was to avoid becoming another animal's meal. The person that learns to watch for and avoid the bear--lives! We are wired for survival. Hypervigilance and preparing for dangerous situations is adaptive for survival. So I believe PTSD, as well as other mental disorders, are protective and actually keep us alive. You and I wouldn't be here if it weren't for PTSD. I challenge you to discover the silver lining in your situation!

False Alarms: Panic Attacks Explained

Intense feeling of fear or loss of control. Heart beating out of your chest. Panting. Butterfly sensation in your gut. Tingling in your fingers. Trembling. Breaking out in a sweat. Dizziness. Chills or feeling flush.

The above are typical physical responses of panic. Sometimes panic attacks are preceded by a trigger. For me, it happens when I'm driving on the highway and see flashing police lights in my rearview mirror, which is a normal reaction to seeing an emergency vehicle. At other times in my past, panic came from out of the blue.

Why do our bodies react this way? Well, the symptoms of panic are physiologically related to the Fight or Flight Response. In natural settings, this response would ready the body to fight an aggressor or run for survival. Your body immediately responds by dumping adrenaline into your blood stream. This results in rapid breathing, racing heart beats, a blood sugar spike and blood rushing from your digestive system to your muscles. Again, this is a natural response for survival.

In Panic Disorder, the body's alarm system, the fight or flight response is overly sensitive and triggered when there is no perceived threat. There may be a variety of reasons for your false alarms. It could be due to previous traumas or the fact that today's stressors tend to be more chronic, such as ongoing bills and mortgages; things that hang around a lot longer than a chance encounter with a bear or lion lasting only a few seconds. The modern world has an additional layer of complexity which we have been only living with for a few hundred years. Our brains developed over millions of years. This may help you understand the reason for the false alarm. Also, find ways to lower your stress level. Effective coping tools include daily exercise, deep breathing exercises and quality sleep.

Panic Detector

At the beginning of this book I shared my personal experience with panic attacks. I shared how I discovered my recovery. Again, during the course of writing this book, I found myself dealing with increasing work and personal stress which escalated into a panic attack. Even with my knowledge, recovery work and education, and my daily stress reduction techniques, I still ended up having another panic attack out of the blue after years of absence. So, even I am not immune to relapses. I, too, am on this journey of life and recovery--we all are.

It was as if the heightened awareness, the tingling sensation and whirling thoughts were my body's own "panic detector" or "spider-sense", alerting me to slow down and examine my current life stressors. It was in that moment with that panic attack that I personally realized psychiatric symptoms have meaning. It is up to us to discover the meaning, sometimes alone and sometimes with the help of a therapist. I discovered that when the symptoms happened, especially panic, it was my mind and body's way of telling me to *slow down, stop and review your current stressors.* I am now going to be referring to this as the Panic Police.

So, when you get a message from the Panic Police, do what you would do if you were being pulled over.

1. Slow Down
2. Stop
3. Review

Review what is going on in your life, what is working well and where you need to course correct. In this ever-amazing digital world, we must take time to unplug, slow our minds and listen to ourselves. Remember, if your body is *screaming* at you with a panic attack, that's your cue to slow down and re-train yourself to listen to your body's whispers. Your body knows what it needs. Are you paying attention?

Growth

"It comes to a simple choice, get busy living or get busy dying" – Andy Dufresne

From *The Shawshank Redemption*.

Growth and change: you must move past the guilt and hopelessness. You cannot continue to be a victim of mental illness. What has transpired has passed; don't keep yourself locked in a prison of the past. Moving ahead is what counts. You must face your problem and acknowledge your relationship to it. It may have even served you for a short time, but consider what it is robbing you of and preventing you from experiencing. Anger has a way of shackling you in chains. On the other hand, forgiveness has been shown to reduce levels of depression and anger.[73] Embrace your emotional struggles, learn from them, even thank them, but tell them that you will no longer be a victim and move forward. Make this commitment to yourself and reclaim your life.

My Continual Growth in Recovery

In the course of writing this book, I had a difficult work-related event. It was something that most people in my position would consider a highly stressful scenario. In my attempts to cope with this stressor, I reached out to my mentor. He had dealt with a similar stressful work-related situation, and encouraged me to continue talking about it with close confidantes "until I get bored with it." It was not until a few hours later that I realized the power in his suggestion. He had just prescribed to me a form of psychosocial treatment. The psychological piece being the

143

processing of the information and emotions associated with this situation. But the additional layer, the social layer, was that I would be reaching out and sharing with numerous persons, which would result in the form of interaction and social support during this difficult process. You see, I have been studying recovery for over 6 years, yet, I still benefit from other's perspectives. My recovery has taken its own, non-linear path.

Take it Easy on Yourself

Don't be too hard on yourself. Remember on the winding road of recovery and life, we are going to hit rough spots. We are going to change how we think about these experiences. We are going to reflect on these times of rest before the next growth. Remember the ongoing trials and experiments we performed within our recovery will be our most valuable teachers. You are going to learn what things do not work for you and what things do work, and that is powerful!

In Closing

Thank you for your interest in the recovery process. My mission is to help those around the world experiencing brain disorders learn that they have power over these difficult symptoms. In my clinical work, I am able to help one person at a time. I hope that through this book, I can reach even more individuals, while starting a mental health revolution. By doing this and spreading the word about recovery, you and I together, will be helping the world heal…and thrive…starting with you!

Bibliography

1. https://www.nimh.nih.gov/health/statistics/prevalence/any-anxiety-disorder-among-adults.shtml
2. https://www.nimh.nih.gov/health/statistics/prevalence/any-mood-disorder-among-adults.shtml
3. http://www.who.int/mediacentre/factsheets/fs369/en/
4. Am Psychol. 2007 Feb-Mar;62(2):95-108. Promoting and protecting mental health as flourishing: a complementary strategy for improving national mental health. Keyes CL
5. Neuroimage Clin. 2016 May 14;11:658-66. The volumetric and shape changes of the putamen and thalamus in first episode, untreated major depressive disorder. Lu Y
6. Psychiatry Res. 2013 Sep 30;213(3):179-85. Reduced thalamic volumes in major depressive disorder. Nugent AC
7. Psychol Med. 2012 Apr;42(4):671-81. Meta-analysis of volumetric abnormalities in cortico-striatal-pallidal-thalamic circuits in major depressive disorder. Bora E
8. PLoS One. 2014 Jan 10;9(1):e79055. Frontal-subcortical volumetric deficits in single episode, medication-naïve depressed patients and the effects of 8 weeks fluoxetine treatment: a VBM-DARTEL study. Kong L
9. Neuropsychopharmacology. 2012 Feb;37(3):734-45. Gray matter volumes in obsessive-compulsive disorder before and after fluoxetine or cognitive-behavior therapy: a randomized clinical trial. Hoexter MQ
10. Neurology 2010 July 6:75:35-41. Depressive Symptoms and Risk of Dementia. Saczynksi, J
11. J Neurol Neurosurg Psychiatry. 2004 Dec;75(12):1662-6. Does the risk of developing dementia increase with the number of episodes in patients with depressive disorder and in patients with bipolar disorder? Kessing LV
12. BMC Med. 2013 Sep 12;11:200. So depression is an inflammatory disease, but where does the inflammation come from? Berk M
13. https://en.wikipedia.org/wiki/History_of_mental_disorders
14. https://en.wikipedia.org/wiki/Mental_disorder
15. Psychiatr Serv. 2009 Oct;60(10):1323-8. County-level estimates of mental health professional shortage in the United States. Thomas KC
16. http://www.samhsa.gov/recovery
17. Innovations and Research. 1993; 2: 17–24. Recovery from mental illness: the guiding vision of the mental health system in the 1990s. Anthony WA

18. International Review of Psychiatry. 2002 (14) 245-255. Recovery from schizophrenia: a challenge for the 21st century. Robert Paul Liberman
19. Schizophr Bull. 2010 Jan; 36(1): 94–103. The Schizophrenia Patient Outcomes Research Team (PORT): Updated Treatment Recommendations 2009 Julie Kreyenbuhl
20. J Am Geriatr Soc. 2015 Oct;63(10):2014-22. Does Mode of Contact with Different Types of Social Relationships Predict Depression in Older Adults? Evidence from a Nationally Representative Survey. Teo AR
21. PLoS Med. 2010 Jul 27;7(7) Social relationships and mortality risk: a meta-analytic review. Holt-Lunstad J
22. Geriatr Gerontol Int. 2015 Mar;15(3):341-9. Influence of health locus of control on recovery of function in recently hospitalized frail older adults. Milte CM
23. Cochrane Database Syst Rev. 2011 Jun 15;(6) Psychoeducation for schizophrenia. Xia J
24. Psychiatric Times. 2006 Sept. Preventing Rehospitalization in Schizophrenia. Prince J
25. Int J Soc Psychiatry. 2016 May;62(3):281-91. Uses of strength-based interventions for people with serious mental illness: A critical review. Tse S
26. Psychol Psychother. 2015 Oct 24. Anxiety, depression and autonomy-connectedness: The mediating role of alexithymia and assertiveness. Rutten EA
27. J Caring Sci. 2016 Sep 1;5(3):195-204. The Effect of Mindfulness-integrated Cognitive Behavior Therapy on Depression and Anxiety among Pregnant Women: a Randomized Clinical Trial. Yazdanimehr R
28. J Gen Intern Med.Differential Impact of Homelessness on Glycemic Control in Veterans with Type 2 Diabetes Mellitus. Axon RN
29. Int J Environ Res Public Health. 2017 Jan 9;14(1). Maternal and Child Health of Internally Displaced Persons in Ukraine: A Qualitative Study. Nidzvetska S
30. Gerontologist. 2017 Jan 11. pii: gnw187. Perceived Neighborhood Safety, Social Cohesion, and Psychological Health of Older Adults. Choi YJ
31. Am J Clin Nutr. 2014 Jan;99(1):181-97. A systematic review and meta-analysis of dietary patterns and depression in community-dwelling adults. Lai JS
32. Ann Neurol. 2013 Oct;74(4):580-91. Mediterranean diet, stroke, cognitive impairment, and depression: A meta-analysis. Psaltopoulou T

33. World Psychiatry. 2015 Oct;14(3):370-1. International Society for Nutritional Psychiatry Research consensus position statement: nutritional medicine in modern psychiatry. Sarris J

34. BMC Med. 2017 Jan 30;15(1):23. A randomised controlled trial of dietary improvement for adults with major depression (the 'SMILES' trial). Jacka FN

35. Prim Care Companion J Clin Psychiatry. 2008; 10(6): 440–447. Examining the Efficacy of Adjunctive Aripiprazole in Major Depressive Disorder: A Pooled Analysis of 2 Studies. Michael E. Thase

36. JAMA Intern Med. 2016 Sep 12. Sugar Industry and Coronary Heart Disease Research: A Historical Analysis of Internal Industry Documents. Kearns CE

37. Auto Immun Highlights. 2014 Oct 16;5(2):55-61. Celiac and non-celiac gluten sensitivity: a review on the association with schizophrenia and mood disorders. Porcelli B

38. Front Hum Neurosci. 2016 Mar 29;10:130. Bread and Other Edible Agents of Mental Disease. Bressan P

39. Nutr Metab (Lond). 2009 Feb 26;6:10. Schizophrenia, gluten, and low-carbohydrate, ketogenic diets: a case report and review of the literature. Kraft BD

40. J Atten Disord. 2006 Nov;10(2):200-4. A preliminary investigation of ADHD symptoms in persons with celiac disease. Niederhofer H

41. Schizophr Res. 2015 Dec;169(1-3):491-3. Ketogenic diet reverses behavioral abnormalities in an acute NMDA receptor hypofunction model of schizophrenia. Kraeuter AK

42. Prostaglandins Leukot Essent Fatty Acids. 2017 Apr;119:38-44. Lipid correlates of antidepressant response to omega-3 polyunsaturated fatty acid supplementation: A pilot study. Gananças L

43. Nat Rev Neurosci. 2012 Oct;13(10):701-12. Mind-altering microorganisms: the impact of the gut microbiota on brain and behaviour. Cryan JF

44. Harv Health Lett. 2011 Feb;36(4):3. Mindful eating. Slow down, you're eating too fast. Distracted, hurried eating may add pounds and take away pleasure.

45. Environ Health Perspect. 2016 Aug 23. Polychlorinated Biphenyl and Organochlorine Pesticide Concentrations in Maternal Mid-Pregnancy Serum Samples: Association with Autism Spectrum Disorder and Intellectual Disability. Lyall K

46. Environ Health Perspect. 2016 Jul 25. Prenatal Residential Proximity to Agricultural Pesticide Use and IQ in 7-Year-Old Children. Gunier RB

47. Arch Toxicol. 2016 Oct 8. Pesticides: an update of human exposure and toxicity. Mostafalou S

48. Psychosom Med. 2007 Sep-Oct;69(7):587-96. Exercise and pharmacotherapy in the treatment of major depressive disorder. Blumenthal JA

49. Psychosom Med. 2011 Feb-Mar;73(2):127-33. Exercise and pharmacotherapy in patients with major depression: one-year follow-up of the SMILE study. Hoffman BM

50. Psychosom Med. 2000 Sep-Oct;62(5):633-8. Exercise treatment for major depression: maintenance of therapeutic benefit at 10 months. Babyak M

51. Sports Med. 2010 Sep 1;40(9):765-801. Neuroplasticity - exercise-induced response of peripheral brain-derived neurotrophic factor: a systematic review of experimental studies in human subjects. Knaepen K

52. Br J Sports Med. 2012 Oct;46(13):927-30. Television viewing time and reduced life expectancy: a life table analysis. Veerman JL

53. Circulation. 2016 Sep 19. Pii. Sleep Duration and Quality: Impact on Lifestyle Behaviors and Cardiometabolic Health: A Scientific Statement From the American Heart Association. St-Onge MP

54. J Psychiatr Ment Health Nurs. 2016 Feb;23(1):3-11. Social rhythm interventions for bipolar disorder: a systematic review and rationale for practice. Crowe M

55. Int J Disabil Hum Dev. 2009 Jul;8(3):283-286. Short exposure to light treatment improves depression scores in patients with seasonal affective disorder: A brief report. Virk G

56. Front Psychol. 2016 Jun 30;7:967. Effects of Mindfulness-Based Cognitive Therapy on Body Awareness in Patients with Chronic Pain and Comorbid Depression. de Jong M

57. Adm Policy Ment Health. 2016 Oct 5. Explication and Definition of Mental Health Recovery: A Systematic Review. Ellison ML

58. Can J Public Health. 2016 Oct 20;107(3):e251-e257. Individual- and community-level determinants of Inuit youth mental wellness. Gray AP

59. Biol Psychiatry. 2006 Oct 1;60(7):690-6. Early social enrichment shapes social behavior and nerve growth factor and brain-derived neurotrophic factor levels in the adult mouse brain. Branchi I

60. Psychoneuroendocrinology. 2016 Nov;73:244-251. Common variant in OXTR predicts growth in positive emotions from loving-kindness training. Isgett SF

61. Soc Cogn Affect Neurosci. 2016 Oct;11(10):1579-87. Effects of oxytocin administration on spirituality and emotional responses to meditation. Van Cappellen P
62. Davidson, Larry. The Roots of the Recovery Movement in Psychiatry: Lessons Learned by Jaak Rakfeldt, John Strauss and Larry Davidson. Wiley & Sons. 2010. Print. pg.58.
63. Recovery from Severe Mental Illnesses: Research Evidence and Implications for Practice, Volume 1 by Larry Davidson, Courtenay Harding, and LeRoy Spaniol. Copyright © 2005. Center for Psychiatric Rehabilitation, Trustees of Boston University. (permission granted)
64. https://www.surgeongeneral.gov/library/reports/national-strategy-suicide-prevention/factsheet.pdf
65. Suicide Life Threat Behav. 2016 Aug;46(4):427-46. Factors Associated with Achieving Complete Mental Health among Individuals with Lifetime Suicidal Ideation. Baiden P
66. BMC Psychiatry. 2016 Jul 7;16:216. Effectiveness and cost-effectiveness of a self-management training for patients with chronic and treatment resistant anxiety or depressive disorders: design of a multicenter randomized controlled trial. Zoun MH
67. Psychosomatics. 2016 Sep-Oct;57(5):505-13. Spirituality and Religiousness are Associated With Fewer Depressive Symptoms in Individuals With Medical Conditions. Lucette A
68. Compr Psychiatry. 2016 Oct;70:17-24. Do spirituality and religiousness differ with regard to personality and recovery from depression? A follow-up study. Mihaljevic S
69. Soc Psychiatry Psychiatr Epidemiol. 2016 Sep 8. Causal inference and longitudinal data: a case study of religion and mental health. VanderWeele TJ
70. J Nerv Ment Dis. 2016 Nov;204(11):861-867. Characteristics of Spirituality and Religion Among Suicide Attempters. Mandhouj O
71. Scand J Psychol. 2015 Dec;56(6):700-7. The relationships among gratitude, self-esteem, depression, and suicidal ideation among undergraduate students. Lin CC
72. http://www.ptsd.va.gov/public/PTSD-overview/basics/how-common-is-ptsd.asp
73. Trauma Violence Abuse. 2016 Mar 23. Forgiveness Therapy for the Promotion of Mental Well-Being: A Systematic Review and Meta-Analysis. Akhtar S

Definitions at the beginning of each Elements chapter quoted from Dictionary.com

www.ingramcontent.com/pod-product-compliance
Lightning Source LLC
Chambersburg PA
CBHW021146090426
42740CB00008B/959